Gethsemane

David Hare is one of Britain's most internationally performed playwrights. He was born in Sussex in 1947. Fourteen of his plays have been presented at the National Theatre, including a trilogy about the Church, the Law and the Labour Party – *Racing Demon*, *Murmuring Judges* and *The Absence of War* – which was presented in repertory in the Olivier Theatre in 1993. Ten of his best-known plays, including *Plenty*, *The Secret Rapture*, *Skylight*, *The Blue Room*, *Amy's View*, *The Judas Kiss*, *Via Dolorosa* – in which he performed – and *The Vertical Hour* have also been presented on Broadway.

D0715260

by the same author

PLAYS ONE
(*Slag, Teeth 'n' Smiles, Knuckle, Licking Hitler, Plenty*)
PLAYS TWO
(*Fanshen, A Map of the World, Saigon,*
The Bay at Nice, The Secret Rapture)
PLAYS THREE
(*Skylight, Amy's View, The Judas Kiss, My Zinc Bed*)
THE GREAT EXHIBITION
RACING DEMON
MURMURING JUDGES
THE ABSENCE OF WAR
VIA DOLOROSA
THE BREATH OF LIFE
THE PERMANENT WAY
STUFF HAPPENS
THE VERTICAL HOUR

adaptations
THE RULES OF THE GAME by Pirandello
THE LIFE OF GALILEO by Brecht
MOTHER COURAGE AND HER CHILDREN by Brecht
IVANOV by Chekhov
THE BLUE ROOM from *Reigen* by Schnitzler
PLATONOV by Chekhov
THE HOUSE OF BERNARDA ALBA by Lorca
ENEMIES by Gorky

screenplays for television
LICKING HITLER
DREAMS OF LEAVING
HEADING HOME

screenplays
DAVID HARE COLLECTED SCREENPLAYS
(*Wetherby, Paris by Night, Strapless,*
Heading Home, Dreams of Leaving)
PLENTY
THE SECRET RAPTURE
THE HOURS

opera libretto
THE KNIFE

prose
ACTING UP
ASKING AROUND: BACKGROUND TO THE DAVID HARE TRILOGY
WRITING LEFT-HANDED
OBEDIENCE, STRUGGLE AND REVOLT

DAVID HARE

Gethsemane

faber and faber

First published Great Britain in 2008
by Faber and Faber Limited
3 Queen Square, London WC1N 3AU

Typeset by Country Setting, Kingsdown, Kent CT14 8ES
Printed in England by CPI Bookmarque, Croydon, Surrey

A CIP record for this book
is available from the British Library

ISBN 978–0–571–24529–1

2 4 6 8 10 9 7 5 3 1

For Joe, Lewis, Darcy and Candice

Gethsemane received its first production in the Cottesloe auditorium of the National Theatre, London, on 4 November 2008. The cast, in order of appearance, was as follows:

Lori Drysdale Nicola Walker
Mike Drysdale Daniel Ryan
Frank Pegg Pip Carter
Otto Fallon Stanley Townsend
Meredith Guest Tamsin Greig
Suzette Guest Jessica Raine
Monique Toussaint Gugu Mbatha-Raw
Geoff Benzine Adam James
Alec Beasley Anthony Calf

Director Howard Davies
Designer Bob Crowley
Costume Designer Fotini Dimou
Lighting Designer Mark Henderson

Gethsemane is my third recent play at
the National Theatre drawing on public events.
The Permanent Way was pure fact, transcribed.
Stuff Happens was one-third transcribed, two-thirds
imagined. *Gethsemane* is pure fiction.

DH

Characters

Lori Drysdale

Mike Drysdale

Frank Pegg

Otto Fallon

Meredith Guest

Suzette Guest

Monique Toussaint

Geoff Benzine

Alec Beasley

GETHSEMANE

For what I want to do, I do not do.
But what I hate, I do.

Romans 7

Act One

ONE

Lori Drysdale stands alone. She is in her thirties, well dressed, with dark hair.

Lori For some reason I can't explain to you, people believe in a book. They choose to believe in one book. They find a book and they decide they believe in it. In this book, they say, all wisdom resides. Different people choose different books, most of them according to where they were born. They hold up the book. 'Everything that is true,' people say, 'is in this book.'

Who, then, are we? The rest of us? The people who say, 'Perhaps.' Or, 'Explain to me, please.' Or, 'Well, I'm not sure.' Who are we?

We are the people without a book.

TWO

A rush of good music. The stage changes shape to suggest an office lobby. Frank Pegg appears. He is thin, willowy, ginger-haired, in his late twenties. He moves to shake hands with Mike Drysdale, who is approaching from the opposite side. Mike is thickset, in his early thirties, a rugby player. They are both in suits.

Frank You won't meet him for long. You know he can't see you for long.

Mike I didn't expect to meet him for long. I wasn't expecting to meet him at all.

Frank What do you know about pop music?

Mike Honestly?

Frank Yes.

Mike I know very little.

Frank That's fine.

Mike Except that it's not called pop, any more, is it?

Otto Fallon appears. He is in his sixties, his hair in a ponytail, cufflinks flashing, with an air of unforced wealth.

Otto Good morning. You're Mike Drysdale.

Mike You're Otto Fallon.

Otto That's right. Ask me anything you like.

Mike I ask you?

Otto By all means.

Mike I was expecting you to ask me.

Otto Oh, please!

Otto smiles. The idea is ridiculous.

First I want to apologise for bringing you in at this hour.

Mike It's all right. I'm an early riser.

Otto Something sad about us, isn't there? The early morning people. What time is it?

Frank Just gone seven.

Otto We're rather sad, aren't we? How wonderful it would be to lie in bed till ten, eating toast. Toast with butter. That would be stylish. But in us there's a sort of admission, desperate isn't it? If we don't get up at the crack, we won't get up at all.

Mike I've always done it.

4

Otto What?

Mike Got up early.

Otto looks at him thoughtfully.

Otto Jolly boating weather.

Mike I'm sorry?

Otto We've never had anyone from university before, have we, Frank? Let alone Oxford.

Mike Cambridge.

Otto What a interesting life you must have led.

Mike Not at all. No. No, actually it's been dullish. I *was* briefly in the police . . .

Otto Frank mentioned that. What motivated you? Why to be a policeman?

Mike I don't know. There was graduate entrance. And I don't mean to sound highfalutin, but perhaps a sense of injustice.

Otto A sense of injustice. Excellent. We like that. Why should people just be defined by their function? No, no. Let them have feelings, let them have thoughts.

Mike Well, whatever. I was uncomfortable in the police. Since then I've been working in the Home Office.

Otto Yes.

Otto looks hard, considering him.

Frank and I didn't go to university, did we, Frank?

Frank No.

Otto No such luck. What is it I always say?

Frank You're looking at me.

Otto Why not? Mr Drysdale hasn't heard it.

Frank That doesn't mean I have to repeat it. Is that what I'm here for? To repeat things you can't be bothered to say?

But nevertheless Frank turns to Mike.

Otto always says he was educated in the university of life.

Otto There! Have you ever heard that expression before?

Mike Well, as a matter of fact . . .

Otto I know, it's wonderful, isn't it? The school of rough knocks. So. How come the Home Office?

Mike Oh well, actually, I went in as a temp, a temporary job, and I rose.

Otto You rose at speed?

Mike The standard isn't high.

Otto That's what they say.

Mike I joined one week because I could work a computer, next week I was answering the minister's mail.

Otto Yes. Interesting.

He looks straight at Mike.

We ourselves are in the music business. Popular music. In recent years the company's brief has expanded. We've taken on duties of a political nature. Of a broad political nature.

Mike What duties?

Otto doesn't answer.

You rang last night, you said it was urgent.

Otto It is urgent.

Mike Forgive me, I'd barely even heard of you.

Otto That's fine. Fewer people have heard of me the better. These days it's smart to be anonymous, don't you think? There's nothing more vulgar than being famous. And glamour isn't even glamorous any more. Take it from me.

Mike Is that the world you move in?

Otto Rich, yes. Famous, yes. Fascinating, I don't think so.

Otto flashes his smile at Mike.

I was going to ask: do you know anything about music?

Mike Not much.

Otto Don't worry, it's not a disqualification.

Mike My wife knows more. She's working as a busker, in fact.

Otto A busker?

Mike Just at the moment. At Barons Court. Again, it's a temporary thing.

Otto It's not a lifelong thing?

Mike No. Temporary.

Otto And is she doing well, your wife?

Mike Well, there's a structure to busking.

Otto There's a structure to everything.

Mike Yes. But in particular it depends on the pitch. I don't mean the pitch of the music . . .

Frank Obviously.

Mike Pitch meaning the place where you play.

Frank We knew that's what you meant. Clearly. We're not idiots.

Otto There's a hierarchy?

Mike Yes.

Otto And is there violence?

Mike I don't know. I really don't know. There may be violence. Elsewhere. At other stations. But Lori's been very careful.

Otto Choosing where to play?

Mike That's it.

Otto Not stealing spots that belong to other people?

Mike Well, of course Lori doesn't do that.

Otto And you're at peace with it, are you? Your wife being out? Being out at night?

Mike She doesn't play nights.

Otto You wouldn't let her?

Mike It's up to her.

Mike looks, firm about this.

Otto Be clear: there's not a breath of criticism.

Mike I didn't take it as criticism.

Otto Don't mistake me: I was a hairdresser, I'm all for women's liberation. The more liberated the better. I spent many years listening to women's conversation. Because that's how I started out. In Hendon. I was a hairdresser in Hendon. Did you know that?

Mike I read it.

Otto Does it surprise you?

Mike No, because I read it.

Otto Listen to women for any length of time, listen to what they say, especially to each other, and your respect for them will grow. I cut hair for five years and at the end my respect was boundless. Time spent listening to women is never wasted. Compare it with men's conversation.

Frank Footling.

Otto Yeah. Women have their priorities right.

He smiles, all charm.

I don't know you, Mike. I don't know your wife. Out evenings. Playing on the Tube. If you're at peace with that. But my wife's at home, preparing for Sunday lunch.

Otto looks, shrewd now.

In a meritocracy the man who's full of merit ought to be the man who rises. Why else call it a meritocracy? And if it's not a meritocracy, what is it?

Mike Honestly, I do OK. I'm not complaining.

Otto No. But you're struggling to pay the mortgage. Children?

Mike No.

Frank Anyone want coffee?

Mike Thank you.

Frank glides out, silent.

Just so you understand: my wife did have a job, but she left. Voluntarily.

Otto What sort of job?

Mike She was a teacher. She taught. That's what she did. For the moment, busking's a choice.

9

Otto It's your wife's choice?

Mike Forgive me, you have a way of saying 'your wife'.

Otto Do I?

Mike As if a woman were some sort of possession.

Mike concedes.

All right, fair enough, sufficient to say – I don't know why I'm even saying this: the fact is, I admit it, we got in over our heads.

Otto Buying a house?

Mike Yes. Buying a house in London. Then my wife walked out of her job.

Otto looks at him a moment.

Otto Yes. Life's fun, isn't it? Until it isn't. Is that how it was?

Mike chooses to be direct at last.

Mike Just tell me, so I understand. Tell me what I'm doing here.

Otto It's simple. I'm saying, look at you, Mike. I know people in the Home Office. They say you're good. You're very good. Someone I know was talking about a meeting you had with the minister. It was ridiculous. You knew so much more than the minister did.

Mike Yes, well, be fair, the minister's a busy woman. She has many briefs. I have one.

Otto This person told me you ran rings round her.

Mike I don't think that's true.

Otto You knew so much more than she did, it was embarrassing.

Mike Only about asylum.

Otto They were at a meeting, they were sitting there, they thought, 'Hello, this is something new, this is interesting. The lettuce is eating the rabbit.'

Frank comes in silently and sets down three small brown plastic cups of espresso.

Frank Coffee.

Mike Thank you.

Otto turns, decisive.

Otto Yes, there is a job. I asked you here to offer you a job. You'd be paid by an offshore company. You'd have to let me know if that's a problem for you.

Mike I would pay tax, I hope?

Otto Certainly. Certainly you'd pay tax.

Mike Good. Because I couldn't contemplate not paying tax.

Otto I appreciate that.

Mike I couldn't contemplate any kind of arrangement which was in any way off-colour.

Otto Everyone here pays tax. Without exception. Unless they have a very good reason not to. Take something out, put something back, that's a principle I've always believed in. We're citizens, not consumers. With rights come obligations.

Otto takes a sip of coffee.

Mike What is the job exactly?

Otto What is it?

Mike Yes.

Otto Raising money. That's what we do. We raise money.

Mike You mean, for the government?

Otto Hardly, no. For the party.

Mike The party?

Otto Yes. There is a difference, you know. We're always looking for new ways of raising money. Identifying new targets. That'll be nine-tenths of your work. Frank'll be clearer. Frank'll work out the details. Not that you'll work to Frank. You'll work to me.

Frank Nobody works to me.

Otto Nobody works to Frank because his fat heart is even bigger than his fat head.

Frank seems fine with this.

As to salary, we can discuss it, but in broad terms, go home, take a pair of scissors, open your wallet, cut up the green, order a gold. Everyone happy?

Frank I'm always happy.

Otto has put his coffee down and is about to leave. Mike is momentarily alarmed.

Mike Can I ask one question?

Otto Yes.

Mike You said someone was at a meeting.

Otto Yes.

Mike They recommended me.

Otto Yes.

Mike I'd like to know who that person was. Meetings at that level are confidential. I'd like to think that when I speak to a minister it's in confidence.

Otto Quite right. You're right to expect that. And I respect you for it. Matter of fact, it was the minister. She told me. She's a friend of mine.

THREE

Frank, alone.

Frank The usual thing is to offer chicken and salmon. I know how the thinking goes: there's nobody who doesn't like chicken or salmon. The fact is, though, that the people who like chicken are the very same people who also like salmon. That's the flaw in the thinking. You're playing to the lowest common denominator.

Between April and October, I can ring Ladbrokes before attending any charity event, any sporting event, any wedding, any funeral, and I will wager my house, my car and my sister's virtue that there's going to be salmon. And I never lose. Myself, I never offer salmon. I just wouldn't do it. And I never offer chicken. I don't offer watercress either, or small pieces of dill which nobody likes and nobody eats. If God wanted fish to be served in jelly, he would have given the recipe in the Book of Revelation. And if you want to know something really disgusting, it's cold pasta salad. I offer gull's eggs, a simple salad niçoise, a good white burgundy, and if you can spatchcock a quail and barbecue it over hot coals in a simple marinade, then people generally cheer up no end. People want to be cheerful. And if you can help them to be cheerful, why give them salmon?

FOUR

Another rush of good music. The set shimmers, turns and becomes an office with a central desk, a computer on it.

Meredith Guest is close to fifty, smart and well-tailored. Suzette is sixteen, sitting on a desk in dark tights and a micro-skirt. Monique Toussaint is black, from the French West Indies, in her late twenties, also suited.

Meredith So you're not going to tell me? You're not going to tell me why you did it?

Suzette is unapologetic.

Suzette Why do you think I did it? Why do you think I did it?

Meredith Well, I've listened to a series of reasons, I can't say at the end of it I really understand.

Suzette That isn't my problem. That's yours.

Meredith Very well. Monique's been listening . . .

Monique I have . . .

Meredith Monique's been listening as well. Maybe she understands you better than me.

Suzette She certainly knows me better than you.

Meredith All right, Suzette, very funny.

Suzette She spends more time with me.

Meredith That's an exaggeration, as well you know.

Suzette And she listens when I speak. I say something, Monique says something immediately afterwards, and the two bear some relation. They relate. One has something to do with the other. Whereas when you speak, it's about what you're already thinking, it's never about what I've just said.

Suzette grins. Neither can take it seriously.

Meredith All right.

Suzette And by the way – and this is just a by the way – *by the way*, if you really cared about me, you wouldn't have Monique here in the first place. But of course in your job you're scared to be alone in a room with anyone.

Meredith That isn't true.

Suzette Especially your own daughter.

Meredith rolls her eyes.

Meredith Monique is here, as you well know, because what you've done needs handling.

Suzette Handling?

Meredith I need professional advice.

Suzette What, I suppose you're going to tell me I haven't hurt myself, I've hurt the whole family? Only as usual family means you.

Monique She's quick, isn't she?

Meredith Well, nobody ever said she lacked a sense of humour.

Suzette Oh yeah. And since that's what we're talking about . . .

Meredith That's not what we're talking about . . .

Suzette Has it ever occurred to you, my sense of humour, that may be the very reason I don't have a boyfriend?

Meredith Oh God . . .

Monique Please, I do think, Suzette . . .

Meredith This is way, way off-subject.

Suzette Interesting, isn't it? I don't have a boyfriend precisely because boys are terrified of jokes. Who owns the comedy circuit? Duh!

But Meredith is already shaking her head.

Meredith I'm not going to rise to this . . .

Suzette Why not?

Meredith Because it's not what we're here to talk about.

Suzette That's so typical, that's so fucking typical . . .

Meredith But as a matter of fact, what are you saying? What are you actually saying? Shall we stop to interrogate this? You can't get a boyfriend because you're too witty, you're too *witty*, is that your reasoning? And somehow you think this is *our* fault?

Suzette Listen: if you listen, I didn't say I can't get a boyfriend.

Meredith Didn't you?

Suzette I didn't say I *can't* get a boyfriend. I said I *don't* have a boyfriend. Isn't English your first language? 'Can't' and 'don't' are different. I could but I don't.

Meredith And the boys you have brought home are romantic wrecks. Jesus Christ!

She despairs at the memory.

And this – what? – this being-too-witty problem somehow relates to your drugs problem, does it?

Suzette I don't have a drugs problem. I take drugs. How is that a problem?

Meredith It's a problem for me.

Suzette Everything's a problem for you.

Meredith All right. All right – calm down, let's go slower, let's stick to the subject – then tell me this: if you don't have a problem, why did you take drugs?

Suzette Isn't it obvious?

Meredith No. It's not obvious. If it were obvious, I wouldn't ask.

Suzette Why do you think? Why do most people take drugs?

Meredith I don't know. You tell me.

Suzette Because most other people take drugs. That's why.

Meredith To be like other people? People take drugs to be like other people?

Suzette For that very reason. Like – I don't know – most people wear clothes. So people don't point at them on the Tube and say, 'She's got nothing on.'

Meredith And that's the motivation?

Suzette It's a fact. It's a fact, is all.

Meredith Look I'm going to deal with this, I'm going to say –

Suzette You say what you like . . .

Meredith All right, just deal with this, as follows: we gave you a private education –

Suzette I didn't ask for it . . .

Meredith We sent you, your sister, your brother, all of you, to hugely expensive schools, you live a hugely privileged life, we surround you with art and beautiful things, you travel abroad, and at the end of it, all you can say is, 'I want to be like everyone else.'

Suzette Well?

Meredith You do it because everyone else does it, is that your defence?

Suzette It's everyone's defence.

Meredith The difference being not everybody's mother is the Home Secretary. Monique?

Monique crosses her arms, calm.

Monique It's perfectly containable.

Meredith You think so?

Monique Of course. It can be contained.

Meredith That doesn't make it right.

Monique I'm not saying it's right.

Meredith It isn't right.

Monique I'm not *judging*.

Meredith Good.

Monique I'm not here to judge. I'm not interested in whether sixteen-year-old girls should do drugs. What does interest me is how to contain the damage when they do.

Meredith How? How, exactly?

Monique looks straight at Meredith.

Monique The headmistress is a party supporter. She supports the party. She's a big fan of our educational reforms.

Meredith So she should be.

Monique She likes them.

Meredith Good.

Monique She feels the government's going in the right direction.

Meredith Good. Recall her name.

Monique Irene.

Meredith That's right. Irene.

Monique And what's more, Irene's a headmistress, she knows which side her bread is buttered.

Meredith And it's Normandy butter.

Monique Spread thick.

Meredith I write the cheques. I know it's thick.

Monique She doesn't want her school in the papers.

Meredith Have you spoken to her?

Monique gives her a pointedly blank stare.

When did you speak to her?

Monique I didn't speak to her personally.

Meredith Who did speak to her? What did they say?

Monique is without expression. Then:

What about the other girl?

Monique Yes.

Meredith The girl she was with?

Monique Yes.

Suzette Her name's Leticia.

Meredith My daughter goes to school with someone called Leticia?

Suzette And before you ask, her parents are borderline Lib Dems who were against the war. They have positive views on immigration. They're not going to do *you* any favours.

Meredith All right.

Suzette Or any of your lot. They don't *like* you.

Meredith turns to Monique.

Meredith Well?

Monique Also been spoken to. Also fixed.

Meredith Who fixed them?

Again, Monique is blank.

Who fixed them?

Silence.

Monique . . .

Monique Meredith, there are things you don't need to know. Then when people ask you questions you can say, 'I don't know.'

Meredith Well, I *don't* know.

Monique You can say 'I don't know' and you won't be lying.

Suzette Can I do that?

Meredith Can you shut up?

Suzette When people ask me things, can I say 'I don't know. And I'm not lying'?

Meredith turns, vengeful.

Meredith All right, Suzette, you think this is funny . . .

Suzette Well, it is quite funny . . .

Meredith You think this whole thing is grist to your groundbreaking sense of humour, but I took political flak, remember? I took political risks, taking you out of a comprehensive . . .

Suzette Why? Why did you take me out? I didn't want to go.

Meredith To put you, God forgive me, in a decent school . . .

Suzette What you call 'decent'.

Meredith I paid a price, remember?

Suzette Oh, *you* paid a price?

Meredith Because, as far as I'm concerned, you don't deny to any child the chance to find out about Western literature and Western values and Western ideas. If you could give a child that gift, why would you not? What would you say? 'Oh no, I prefer ignorance'? When life can be immeasurably expanded. Immeasurably improved.

Meredith is showing genuine conviction.

Your father and I were happy to do it, and what's more we'd do it again.

Suzette You feel strongly.

Meredith I do.

Suzette I know you feel strongly. But the school you describe doesn't exist. It doesn't exist. It's in your head.

Suzette looks at her mother a moment.

Mum, I don't want to spoil your world picture . . .

Monique Minister, I'm not sure we have time.

Suzette But wait one. The comprehensive wasn't that bad.

Meredith OK. I know you thought that.

Monique We're ninety minutes behind.

Suzette It really wasn't that bad. There were a lot of good teachers . . .

Meredith Lori Drysdale, I suppose.

Suzette Yes, Lori Drysdale.

Meredith Again.

Suzette And the private school isn't so marvellous.

Meredith So you say.

Suzette It's just that you have this fantasy, Mum.

Meredith What fantasy is that?

Suzette That we're all sitting in sw7 reading great literature and working out the world's problems and how to engage with the challenge of Islam and how does feeble democracy fight powerful dictatorship, and actually we're not. We're not. None of us are. Nobody is. However much you pay.

Suzette shrugs slightly.

I'm all for that stuff. Really. I am. But culture's something you buy, isn't it? Like a handbag. It's about status. It doesn't change how you live. It doesn't affect your life. Does it?

Meredith looks at her, thoughtful now.

Meredith I think, Suzette, you and I need to spend some time together.

Suzette It's fine by me.

Meredith I'm going to take you out. We're going to go for a nice Chinese and I'm going to talk to you. About values.

Monique When are you going to do that?

Meredith Tonight. I'm going to do it tonight.

Monique Minister, community policing.

Meredith All right, I'll do it tomorrow night.

Monique Young offenders!

Meredith All right, I'll do it at the weekend. Whatever! I'll do it!

Meredith is firm. She turns to Monique.

Bring me the prospectus. Bring me the school prospectus.

Monique Why? Why am I to bring it?

Meredith Because I'm telling you to.

Monique You don't want to see it.

Meredith I do.

Meredith looks at her a moment. No response.

Monique, I do want to see it.

Monique I don't have a copy to hand.

Meredith I don't believe you, Monique. You have a copy of everything.

Monique You really don't want to see it, Meredith. I promise you. You don't.

Meredith doesn't budge.

You're angry, Minister, and because you're angry you're about to do something foolish. Because it's your own family, because it's your immediate family, you're going to behave in a way you would never normally behave. You're too *smart* to behave.

Meredith So?

Monique All right, the government's not going to fall because of this, not today it isn't, but on the other hand if this gets out, if the news gets out, it can wobble, it can shake. We can avoid all sorts of danger if you don't look at the prospectus. There's only one safe place for a politician to live and that's in ignorance.

Meredith I still want to look at it.

Monique I advise against it.

Meredith I value your advice, Monique.

Monique It's in my office.

Meredith Then go.

Monique doesn't move.

Go.

Monique goes out, angry.

Suzette I don't understand. What's the big drama? What's going on?

Meredith I'm teaching you a lesson.

Suzette What sort of lesson?

Meredith Which your fancy school doesn't teach.

Suzette Then tell me.

Meredith In politics, as in life, real friends are hard to find. The last place to look for them is within your own party.

Suzette I don't understand. What the hell does that mean?

Meredith You behave as you do because you know you'll get away with it. You, Suzette, behave as you wish because whenever you make a mess you can be sure there's someone around to clear it up. And that's what it means to be middle-class.

Meredith looks down, steely.

Have you ever asked yourself why I went into politics?

Suzette So you could lock up Arabs?

Meredith No, not so I could lock up Arabs.

Suzette Because that seems to be what you're doing, mostly.

Meredith No, as it happens, I went into politics for rather more high-minded reasons. To make a difference.

Suzette And you think you're doing that?

Meredith As a matter of fact, I do. And there are quite a lot of us who feel the same thing. The problem is that nobody believes us.

Suzette I wonder why.

Meredith Nobody believes that anyone can choose to be in public life for the public good. And because they don't trust us, they hold us to some ridiculous standard they themselves couldn't possibly meet.

Suzette What's this? Are you feeling sorry for yourself?

Meredith No.

Suzette Sorry for politicians?

Meredith No.

Suzette Well then, Mother?

Meredith I'm not sorry for anyone, I'm telling you how it is. Any idiot can go off for a night and sleep with the boss's wife and it doesn't matter. What does it matter? Nobody cares. It's a night. It's forgotten. But if one of us sleeps with the boss's wife we're all over the papers and we're a laughing stock. That's the difference. It's an organised hypocrisy and it's called democracy.

Monique returns.

Well?

Monique waits, sullen.

Well?

Still Monique does not move.

Did you find the prospectus?

Monique I did.

Meredith Where is it?

Monique It's in my hand.

Meredith Why don't you go to the page where the governors are listed?

Monique What an extraordinary coincidence. It's at that page.

Monique holds it out, without enthusiasm.

Meredith Tell me, do I have a rare sense of the paranormal? Hey, maybe I'm psychic. How long has Otto Fallon been a governor of the school?

Monique says nothing.

Meredith How long?

Monique It doesn't say.

Meredith Longer than a week? Longer than a day?

Monique Don't ask.

Meredith I'm asking. I would like to be reassured.

Monique I'm sure you would.

Meredith What I'm asking: you didn't put him in specially to deal with this?

Monique He was not been put in specially to deal with this. Otto has an intense interest in education. You know that. Education is one of Otto's defining interests. He has long believed that no child should be left behind. Especially the Home Secretary's. For that reason he used his influence

26

as a governor of the school to make sure the school's reputation was protected.

Meredith turns to her daughter.

Meredith And so there's your lesson. There you have it.

Suzette is furious, searching for a reaction.

Suzette I hate you.

Meredith I know. I know you hate me.

Suzette Everybody hates you.

Meredith It isn't true.

Suzette The whole country hates you. Majorly.

Meredith I don't think so.

Suzette They hate everything about you. Because you're corrupt.

Meredith We're not corrupt. We're careful.

Suzette And there's a difference?

Meredith The first time she met you, Monique said to me, 'Your daughter is an accident waiting to happen.'

Suzette Thank you, Monique.

Meredith So it seems, typically, she made provision. Because that's Monique's job. To foresee the future. Once it was possible to do good by being good. Now the only way to do good is by being clever.

Suzette You think this is clever?

Meredith I do.

Suddenly Meredith raises her voice.

You don't even like dope! You don't even like drugs! What the hell were you doing?

Suzette is cornered, provoked.

Suzette I hate you. I hate you because there isn't any event in our lives that isn't about you.

Monique Now come on.

Suzette If I smoke dope, it's about you. If Daddy has an affair, it's about you.

Monique Is Jack having an affair?

Meredith Not that I know about.

Suzette Can you imagine how tiring that is? Can you imagine what it's like to live with that?

Meredith looks at her, then shakes her head.

Meredith I have to work now. I have to go back to work.

Suzette Why? Why do you have to work?

Meredith Because that's how it is.

Suzette Is it?

Meredith Yes.

Suzette Why?

Meredith We all work harder and harder and to less and less effect. Everyone does. Everything that once was easy has now become difficult. Harold Macmillan read Trollope and walked the moors. We just work. There it is. We try to be as boring as we can because boring is the only safe thing to be.

Meredith looks at Suzette fondly.

We'll talk again soon.

Suzette When?

Meredith Soon.

Suzette But when? When do I next see you? When I next threaten your government?

Meredith reaches out her hand to touch her daughter's cheek. Suzette recoils.

Meredith You hate me today, Suzette. But you won't always hate me. Will you?

FIVE

Monique, alone.

Monique What's my job? Easy. My job is to plan. What any good adviser does is to stand one step back. You analyse. It's easy to predict the mistakes a politician will be tempted to make. You see them coming. The open road and at the end, the yawning elephant trap. That's why you're there. You're able to warn, you're able to advise the minister: 'See that thing over there? At the end of the road? It's an elephant trap.' That's what I do. I identify elephant traps. That's my job. And then usually, most of the time, I stand and watch the minister fall right in.

SIX

Music. A squash court, and the area in front of it. Mike is playing with Otto, both in white shorts and shirts. Mike is running around much more than Otto, sweat pouring down his face. He loses a final point. The two of them move across to pick up towels.

Otto You're never going to learn.

Mike I'm never going to learn unless you teach me.

Otto In that case you're never going to learn.

Mike Why not?

Otto Why would I teach you?

Mike Why wouldn't you?

Otto Because then you'll beat me. I don't want that. I don't want to lose. Ever.

Mike sits exhausted. Otto shrugs as if this is what he had expected.

Mike How do you do it? You stand in the middle of the court, you don't move. You're an old man.

Otto That's the reason. I'm not able to move. And so I don't.

Mike I'm running around like an idiot, and you're standing still.

Otto I turn a handicap into an advantage.

Mike What's so annoying is, I'm cleverer than you are. You know nothing. What do you know about?

Otto Boy bands.

Mike And yet you stand still.

Lori comes in. She's in a coat, carrying car keys.

Otto This must be your wife.

Lori It is. Lori . . .

Otto Three months he's been working here . . .

Lori How do you do? I've heard a lot about you.

Otto And I've never met you. He must have been hiding you.

Mike stands, sweaty, embarrassed. But Lori does not seem intimidated.

I thought you'd be carrying your instrument.

Lori Very funny.

Otto I did say to Mike, it's a brave man who lets his wife play music on the underground railway.

Mike I told you, I don't 'let' her do anything.

Lori I'm surprised you talk about me.

Otto Continually.

Mike Never. He's making it up. It's his method. It's his technique.

Otto I have bad news – I'm afraid I've just thrashed your husband at squash. I have the advantage that it is my court.

Lori Does that make a difference?

Otto I built it.

Lori Personally?

Otto Correct.

Lori To your specifications?

Otto Or rather my architect built it. For years when you said 'architect' everyone spat. Architecture was the most despised of professions. Now for some reason – somebody explain – it's the most fashionable. Why?

Lori I have no idea.

Otto He built my restaurant too. Same fellow. Do you play? Have you played?

Lori Never.

Otto You're more the artistic type.

He flashes a gleaming smile.

I employed Mike, but really it was you I wanted. Employing Mike was a way of getting to you.

Lori Mike told me that.

Otto But of course. I'm sure he tells you everything.

Lori He does.

Otto You're married.

Frank comes in, as always neatly dressed, carrying a couple of bottles.

Ah, Frank, you haven't met Lori.

Frank No.

Otto If I may call you Lori?

Lori Hello, Frank.

Frank Lori. Welcome. We have a white Burgundy. We have a modest Shiraz.

Otto I'm standing here realising just how lucky Mike is.

Frank Fruity, but not screaming fruit. Otto has a vineyard in France.

Otto Even though I don't drink.

Frank That's the paradox.

Otto He hands me a glass, I forget it's there.

Frank You know Otto. He's happier with a joint.

Otto All my interest goes into the label, you see. Specially commissioned. Nothing's pleased me more in recent years than the revival in British art.

Lori British art?

Otto That's right.

Lori You're pleased, are you? By its revival?

Otto I love British art. So negative! So don't-give-a-damn!

Lori Why does that please you?

Otto Everything makes a show of believing in things. You have to believe! Now here are these wonderful young British artists who believe in nothing. Nothing at all! Marvellous!

Lori Yes. Yes. Just a shame you don't drink, really.

Otto gives her his most charming smile.

Otto Your husband did warn me.

Lori What did he warn you of?

Otto Your satirical tongue. He says the blade of your wit was sharpened in a school.

Frank Are you having wine?

Lori I would like a glass, yes. The one that's fruity but not screaming.

Frank You have it. And I'm going to smear a little *foie gras* on toast.

Frank goes out.

Mike Shall I get changed? Shall I shower?

Otto By all means. Shower.

Mike goes out. Otto has sat down on the bench and is considering Lori.

So? School?

Lori What can I say? I was a teacher, yes.

Otto Where?

Lori In Shepherd's Bush.

Otto And were you a happy teacher?

Lori For the hours I was allowed to teach. Do you know much about schools?

Otto Not much. I think I may be a governor here and there, that's all.

Lori Well, teachers don't do much teaching these days.

Otto They're not free? Not free to do what they want?

Lori nods.

What did you teach?

Lori I taught music.

Otto Ah yes. Did you want to be a professional musician?

Lori At one time.

Otto What happened?

Lori I played for a while but I wasn't good enough.

Otto How did you know?

Lori I was full of feelings I wanted to express. Things that couldn't be said.

Otto I don't understand. What can't be said?

Lori What I mean is: things that couldn't be spoken.

Otto Oh, I see. Things beyond sense?

Lori nods. Otto thinks about it.

Well. So what did you play?

Lori Piano. I played piano.

Otto Beautifully?

Lori Not beautifully enough. When I played the sound that came out wasn't the sound I wanted. It was there in my head, but it wasn't in my fingers. So I turned to teaching. I wanted children to feel how powerful music could be.

Otto And did they?

Otto is staring now, considering her.

Lori You just said that in your opinion people nowadays don't believe in anything. But that isn't my experience. Not among children. Not in the comprehensive.

Otto What was your experience?

Lori My impression was that they believed in plenty. They just didn't want to *appear* to believe in anything. That's different, isn't it?

Otto So why did you give up?

Lori I'm sorry?

Otto Why did you leave?

Lori Oh well, it's difficult to explain. I had a sort of Gethsemane.

Otto You're going to have to remind me.

Otto waits.

Please.

Lori It's in the Bible.

Otto That much I know.

Lori It's a night of doubt.

Otto Doubt?

Lori Yes.

Otto What sort of doubt?

Lori As it happens, Christ was sent to do a particular job. He was sent to save the world. And then . . .

Otto What did he want to do instead?

Lori Oh. Anything. He didn't mind. Anything but what was asked of him.

Otto Well, well. What a difficult fellow.

Lori 'Let this cup pass from me.' That's what he said.

Otto And that's what you felt? You felt you'd had enough?

Lori 'His tears fell to the ground like drops of blood.' That's what the Bible says.

Otto And why were you so downhearted?

Lori is reluctant to answer.

All right, fair enough, it's none of my business . . .

Lori Look I'm happy to talk to you about anything you want . . .

At this moment, Frank returns, carrying a plate of foie gras.

Frank Here we are.

Lori I'm not avoiding your question . . .

Frank Laden with goodies.

Otto All I'm saying, it's a shame, I think it's a shame you ducked out, because you're the kind of person who'd succeed at anything.

Lori Yes, but that isn't why I ducked out. I think I *was* succeeding.

Otto You said you admired the children.

Lori I did.

Otto But you never said why.

Lori People say children nowadays have lost their innocence. 'We've robbed children of childhood,' they say. Maybe. But they forget to point out, there is a compensation.

Otto What's that? What's the compensation?

Lori They're clear-eyed. They're not so easily fooled.

Lori has spoken sharply. Frank looks up, catching her tone. Then Otto, as if he had just made up his mind, speaks decisively.

Otto Money's the thing, isn't it?

Lori Is it?

Otto Really. If I'm honest.

Lori Please. Be honest.

Frank He loves saying that. 'Money's the thing.'

Otto People say you need ideals in life. And so you do. But without money, how do you put ideals into practice?

Lori Is it really that simple?

Otto I think it is. Take my own story. From Hendon to Hampstead. A short trip, but a long journey. Self-belief may have given me the route, but money gave me the motor.

Frank Wine?

Lori Thank you.

Frank gives her wine and moves away.

Otto In life it's the first thing you have to accept. Once you accept that, you're on your way. That's why this government's so successful. They accept money. They accept the world. There's only one question worth asking.

'What works?' 'What will work?' That's the only question.
And whatever works – then, right, that's what you must
do.

Lori smiles, amused by him.

Lori Well, I could disagree with you.

Otto I'm sure you could.

Lori But I'm not going to. I'd prefer to wait and see
where you're heading.

Otto You want me to get to the point?

Lori I do.

Otto I'll get to the point. It's this. Let's say, let's say you
gather together all the most capable people in the country,
you put them together in one political party, you can give
that party any name you want. For the sake of argument,
let's call it the Labour Party.

Lori Why not?

Otto Good idea.

Frank Why not?

Otto And that party won't actually have a programme,
it won't *impose* a programme. No, it'll simply deal with
problems as they arise. What's the only question it's
going to ask?

Lori 'What works?'

Otto You're right. That's what it's going to ask.

Lori 'What works?'

Otto I'll put it another way: in my opinion, the people
running the country are capable people. The economy's
doing well. They know what they're doing. Therefore.

Lori Therefore what?

Otto Explain to me why this government shouldn't be in power for ever.

Otto grins, pleased with his provocation. He gets out some papers and starts rolling a joint.

Frank He's hilarious, isn't he?

Otto Frank . . .

Frank I've heard him say lots of crazy things, but I've never heard him say this.

Otto I've said it before.

Frank If he *has* said it before, it certainly wasn't in my presence.

Otto That doesn't mean I haven't said it.

Frank Ooh, now he's tetchy.

Frank holds out the plate.

Foie gras?

Otto All right, let me go on . . .

Frank You know what he's trying to do? You know the point of this?

Lori I have an idea.

Frank He's trying to recruit you. The lifestyle. You get used to it. Good wine.

Frank raises his glass, but Otto is already becoming expansive.

Otto Frank, explain. Mother hen will explain what we do.

Frank Very well, I don't know what Mike has told you.

Lori You're in the fundraising business.

Frank That's what we do.

Otto We raise funds for a political party. As it happens, the Labour Party.

Lori What he hasn't done, really, is tell me how it works.

Otto and Frank smile together. Otto lights his fat joint and takes a deep puff.

Frank Well, we have all sorts of tactics, we try all kinds of ways, but what works best . . .

Otto What generally works best . . .

Frank What Otto will do: he seeks out a client, somebody he's met, say . . .

Otto At a party, say.

Frank That's right. And he talks in a general way.

Otto About general things.

Frank Then, at some point, he says to the client 'Do you want to meet the Prime Minister?'

Otto I slip it into the conversation, so it comes out naturally.

Frank They might be talking about . . . I don't know . . .

Otto Anything.

Frank That's right. Schools. Property prices.

Otto The things you talk about.

Frank He says, 'I've got a house, don't you know? I've got a house in Bishop's Avenue. Do you *know* Bishop's Avenue?'

Otto Chances are, they've heard of it.

Frank Most people have.

Otto It's their idea of everything that's vulgar and disgusting.

Otto and Frank laugh.

Frank So anyway Otto says to the client, 'Come round, have a game of squash, we'll have a game of squash and who knows? Maybe the Prime Minister'll drop by.'

Otto I say, 'He often does, you know.'

Frank Well, you have to admit, it needs character to say no.

Otto People have said no.

Frank Not many.

Otto A few.

Frank So one evening, not long after, they arrive at the house.

Otto They settle down. Nice sofas, deep, nice covers. Hunting scenes.

Frank A few moments later, ring at the door.

Otto 'Oh, come in.' 'Have you met Alec?'

Frank Stone me! It's the Prime Minister.

Otto There he is.

Frank Maybe looking bigger than they expect.

Otto Alec's always just that little bit bigger.

Frank They've seen Alec on telly.

Otto But it's not the same thing.

They both smile. Frank pours himself another glass of wine.

Frank Anyway, Prime Minister blows in, plays a game of squash, takes a shower, towels down, tells the client something he didn't know.

Lori Such as?

Otto Alec says something like, 'The war on terror's much more serious than you think.'

Frank It's good, isn't it?

Otto 'We've got to stop Iran.' Then he goes.

Lori Is that the whole thing?

Frank So that's what's happened.

Lori That's all?

Frank The client's met the Prime Minister, the Prime Minister's told him something he didn't know, if he's lucky he may even have taken a shower with him. Then we ask for money.

Lori How much?

Frank We're not going to waste the Prime Minister's time.

Otto Prime Minister has to come here. He has to drive up from Downing Street. He's not going to do that for less than five figures.

Lori Does anyone ever refuse?

Otto Refuse?

Lori Yes.

Otto You mean not give money? No. I can honestly say no. If you meet the Prime Minister you *always* give money.

Otto, definitive, stubs out his joint.

That's a given.

Frank Sure. That's what the whole thing's based on. Have you met the Prime Minister?

Lori No.

Frank If you met the Prime Minister, *you'd* give him money.

Otto That's how it works.

Frank The whole thing wouldn't work if you met Shirley Bassey.

Lori thinks a moment.

Lori And what else do they get?

Otto What else?

Lori Yes. Is that it? Is that all they get?

Otto No, of course not.

Lori They meet the Prime Minister?

Otto Don't be ridiculous. In return for their money, is what you mean?

Lori Yes. What do they get?

There's a brief silence. Otto looks to Frank.

Otto All right, fair enough, we get the idea, we know what you're asking.

Frank It's not a *protection racket*, if that's what you mean.

Otto You make it sound dishonest. It's not dishonest. Don't believe anything you read.

Frank It's not corrupt.

Otto This is how democracy works. These are intelligent men . . .

Frank They're powerful men. And women. There's a lot of women nowadays. Real women, you know?

Otto It isn't spelt out. I'm not going to spell it out. But obviously, all right? Let's put it this way: if you go to the barbers often enough, then eventually someone's going to give you a haircut.

Mike comes back in a car-coat, gleaming clean, his hair pasted down.

Frank Talking of which . . .

Otto Ah, you're back.

Mike Yes.

Otto Good shower?

Mike Very good, yes.

Otto Look at him. Clean as a pin.

Mike Are you ready to go?

Otto I've been talking to your wife. I've been trying to persuade her to stay.

Mike Stay?

Otto Yes.

Mike Stay for dinner, you mean?

Otto flashes a smile at Frank. There's a sudden silence.

What's going on? Lori?

Lori It's all right, Mike, don't worry, I'm not going to do it.

Otto Aren't you? Why not? Job's good enough for your husband, not good enough for you?

Lori just smiles at his technique.

Enlighten us, Lori. Do you have a reason?

44

Lori I do.

Otto Are you going to tell us what it is?

Lori All sorts of reasons. But – not to be rude – chiefly because everything you've said is wrong.

Otto You mean you disagree with it?

Lori From beginning to end.

Otto Tell me why.

Lori Because, in my view, we're at one of those moments in history. A group of people – yourself included – have taken over the running of things and the rest of us are standing by, powerless, watching, like at a car crash. It's like we're watching a film and we're not enjoying it very much.

Lori stops to look at him a moment.

You say the government claims to believe in 'what works'.

Otto They do.

Lori Well, maybe, but I could point to a couple of wars which don't seem to be working. Not at all. Not at the moment.

Otto Maybe.

Lori And meanwhile – perhaps you haven't noticed – everything may be getting better for some, but it's getting a whole lot worse for most. I don't think this is a government full of practical people, because practical people would address that problem. Sorry, but I think it's a government full of zealots.

Lori gets up to leave.

It's been fun.

Otto Come again.

Lori I enjoyed it.

Otto Me too.

Lori I love your place.

Otto Thank you.

Lori It's grand.

They smile at each other.

Otto I was like you, you know, Lori, for a long time.
I was. Just like you. I spent my youth in mental rioting.
Remember, I never joined the establishment. I didn't have
to. It joined me.

Lori It's been an interesting evening.

Otto Goodnight, Lori.

Frank Lori.

Otto Goodnight, Mike.

Frank and Otto go. Mike and Lori are left.

Mike You like him, don't you?

Lori Of course I like him. What's not to like?

Mike What are you saying?

Lori Me? I'm not saying anything.

Mike All right, then what are you thinking?

Lori I'll tell you what I'm thinking, Mike: I've had a
couple of drinks, d'you mind driving?

Mike No, sure.

Lori And you haven't kissed me hello.

Mike Sorry. I was elsewhere.

He kisses her and puts his arm round her. They go.

SEVEN

Mike, alone, in his car-coat.

Mike I'm not ambitious. There's very little I want. I had an idea early on that I was going to play rugby for England. Then I realised it didn't have to be for England. It was rugby I loved, not dreaming.

I had no expectation of meeting someone like Lori. She had me at 'hello'. Up till then I'd been out with girls who kept rummaging in their handbags and talking to each other. I came to feel like a big wardrobe. Women were glad I was there but that was about it.

I'd love to say the first sight of Lori filled me with joy. But it didn't. We were still students and it filled me with fear. 'Oh my God, I'm going to love this woman. I'm going to love her more than I can bear.' I was amazed when she said 'yes'. I think that's always been the heart of my problem. I can't believe my luck, so I don't trust it.

EIGHT

Music. Everything changes. Lori is in the living room of Meredith's smart Knightsbridge house. Meredith, her armoury of make-up and clothes more perfect than ever, seems to be propelled into the room.

Meredith My goodness, you've come.

Lori It's good to see you.

Meredith It's been a long time.

Lori Yes.

Meredith A very long time. I apologise for all the security. I'm sure you realise, I wouldn't have sought you out if it weren't important.

47

Lori I'm sure.

Meredith smiles, chilly. Nerves are making her sharp.

Meredith This is a concession. You know that? It isn't easy for me to ask.

Lori I understand.

Meredith Every mother believes she can bring up her own child. But I need help. I'll be honest with you. One way or another, this is a difficult moment.

Lori In what way?

Meredith We live on a small island. Sometimes it seems there isn't anyone in the world who doesn't want to get on it.

Lori Oh, I see.

Meredith And I'm the person who has to stop them.

Lori You'll never stop them.

Meredith That's what Suzette says.

Lori Suzette is right.

Meredith Suzette says, 'Mum, it isn't a question of "They're poor and we're rich." It's "They're poor *because* we're rich." And if you can't see that, you can't see anything.'

Lori She's right again.

Meredith Well, as it happens I don't see it. Or rather I can't see it, because I don't have time. I don't have time to see anything or think anything because every hour of the day is taken up. My whole day spent running around trying to padlock the gates at every port and every airport. And at every gate there's a fucking journalist screaming, 'This gate isn't closed. Close this gate.'

Meredith stares, bad-tempered.

Do you read the *Daily Mail*?

Lori No.

Meredith You're right. Nobody reads the *Daily Mail*. But everybody looks at it. You can't read it. It's impossible to read. But that's not what it's there for.

Lori What is it there for?

Meredith To bring down the government.

Meredith forestalls Lori's scepticism.

Oh yes. We do everything they want and still they don't like us.

Lori Perhaps that's why they don't like you. They think you're weak.

Meredith We're not weak, we're strong. Oh, I'm sure you don't think so. Or rather you think it's the wrong kind of strength. Strength without courage.

Lori How do you know what I think?

Meredith Because I used to hear about you. I know all about you.

There's a sudden silence.

A great teacher, Suzette says.

Again, Lori says nothing.

What's that about? Why do the kids like you so much?

Lori I listen to them. And, most of all, I don't call them 'kids'.

Meredith What do you call them?

Lori Children.

Meredith looks shrewdly, assessing her.

Meredith All right, I have to warn you this is a private conversation. It's privileged. Do you know what a private conversation is?

Lori I believe so, yes. One that doesn't appear in the paper tomorrow.

Meredith Exactly. I don't *need* to do this.

Lori Don't you?

Lori waits, but Meredith says nothing.

Shall I go first?

Meredith By all means.

Lori You're having trouble with Suzette?

Meredith Yes.

Lori Where is she?

Meredith Upstairs.

Lori Does she know I'm here?

Meredith Yes. I told her.

Lori You took her out of a school she liked and put her in a school she doesn't like and now she's in open rebellion.

Meredith Yes. She's taking drugs.

Lori What drugs? How often? Who does she take them with?

Meredith shrugs, not knowing.

Meredith With friends.

Lori Do you know their names?

Meredith She's in a set of little girls whose skirts are even shorter than their attention spans. They have witches' covens in their bedrooms and they cast spells by burning copies of *Grazia*.

Lori laughs.

All right, it ought to be funny but it isn't.

Lori Why not?

Meredith Because I believe she genuinely intends to do me harm.

Lori You think it's that serious?

Meredith I know it's serious. I've bred a little viper in a mini-skirt.

Lori is shocked.

Lori Very well, if she hates you so much, the obvious question – why doesn't she speak to her father?

Meredith Do you really want to know?

Lori I do.

Meredith Have you met her father?

Lori shakes her head.

Do you know anything about him? Have you read about him?

Lori Very little.

Meredith All right, to sum up, her father's a hugely interesting man who has a very daring portfolio in certain countries, most of them in the former Soviet bloc. Do you have my meaning?

Lori What are you telling me?

Meredith Jack is not a crook!

Lori I didn't say he was a crook.

Meredith All right. Be clear: Jack is a businessman. He's an entrepreneur. This government has always sought to encourage a business-friendly environment. With great risks come great rewards.

Lori What the hell does that mean?

For the first time Meredith starts to lose it, her temper fraying.

Meredith I don't have to do this, you know. I don't have to do any of it.

Lori I know that.

Meredith I can give up tomorrow and retire to Tuscany.

Lori Are you thinking of retiring?

Meredith I'm not doing it to prove a point. I'm doing it because I believe in it. Everyone thinks we're cynics. We're not. If we were cynics, we'd be out there enjoying ourselves like everyone else. Jesus!

Meredith shakes her head.

Lovely, open the paper every morning. 'Meredith Guest is an idiot.' Marvellous.

Lori I can see.

Meredith On the way to work, I can feel the commuters beneath me, I can feel them, reading their papers and laughing. And why? Because I can't keep out the countless millions. Well no, I can't. Nobody can.

She shrugs, angry.

Oh, I can see of course at some level I'm not easy to live with.

Lori That may well be right.

Meredith All right, to explain: I took her to a Chinese. I took her to the best Chinese.

Lori And?

Meredith I had a night off and I took her out.

Lori How was that?

Meredith I told her she was lucky.

Lori In what way?

Meredith I said, you can light a fire if you want, you can light a fire in the basement and the building will burn. It's that easy. I said, 'You're like all young people. You want it both ways. You want to shake the temple but you don't want to destroy it.'

Meredith thinks back, re-living it.

I said, 'You're spoilt.'

Lori You said that?

Meredith Yes.

Lori What did she say?

Meredith She said, 'You stand for nothing. You represent nothing.'

There is a silence.

Anyway, she's sitting there, she's got a whole sea bass to herself. She's picking at it. And I'm looking at the fucking fish the whole time, her poking with chopsticks, because everything about her annoys me. Like there it is, the most beautiful fish, and she doesn't eat it. I make the gesture, she doesn't accept it.

Lori Because it's just a first step.

Lori is quiet.

When I was teaching I learnt not to judge.

Meredith Judge what?

Lori Between the parents and the children. I met awful parents with wonderful children. I met wonderful parents with awful children. Both.

Meredith is listening now.

In Suzette's case it seems like it may be an issue of loyalty. She believes you care more about the government than you care about her.

Meredith is looking at her. Then Suzette is heard calling from upstairs.

Suzette (*off*) Mum, are you downstairs?

Meredith Yes. I'm downstairs.

Suzette (*off*) Is Lori there?

Meredith Yes. She's longing to see you.

A moment. Then:

Suzette (*off*) Good. I'm coming down.

There is a silence. Meredith is nervous.

Meredith I haven't been honest with you.

Lori In what way?

Meredith I haven't told you the truth. There are two reasons I asked you here. Yes, of course I'd prefer to be friends with my daughter. But also, I have a feeling – I have an instinct. A mother's instinct. Something terrible has happened.

Suzette comes in.

Lori Hi, Suzette.

Suzette Hi, Lori.

Lori You're looking great.

Suzette Thank you. Thank you very much. Long time no see.

There is a moment, the three of them standing, unsure what to do.

My God, they're certainly taking me seriously, aren't they?

Lori They seem to be.

Suzette I'm like all the government's problems. Throw money at them, but they still don't seem to be going away.

Meredith Oh, funny. I'll be upstairs if you need me.

She goes out.

Suzette No, really. Thank you. Thank you for coming.

Lori Not at all.

Suzette You're a friend.

The two women look at each other a moment.

I've been thinking about writing a book. It's going to be called *Words Fail Me*. What do you think?

Lori It's a good title.

Suzette It'll be my first.

Suzette stands there.

You know, like when I'm angry, I can sort of see myself from the outside and I think, 'Oh my God, I'm making a fool of myself.' But that doesn't mean I'm not angry. I *am* angry but I'm also embarrassed. What's the word for that?

Lori Adolescent.

Suzette 'I want to shag that boy but I don't want to wake up with him.' What's the word for that?

Lori Sensible.

They both smile.

Suzette Well, I thought you might know about this.

Lori Would I? How so?

Suzette Because I remember you saying, you used to say music's the highest of the arts –

Lori Ah yes . . .

Suzette – because it doesn't depend on meaning. It can mean anything.

They look at each other a moment.

Get this place, eh? What do you think of it?

Lori It's very nice.

Suzette Yeah, it's nice if you have bad taste. Dad's made a lot of money. Not that I ever see him.

Lori Where's your sister?

Suzette At uni.

Lori Your brother?

Suzette Him too. I'm all on my own-i-o.

Lori shifts.

Lori Suzette, you're far too bright for me to give you a lecture.

Suzette I'd rather have a lecture than a fish.

Lori I'm not going to. But you know why I'm here.

Suzette Mum called you.

Lori Yes. She needs to know what's happened.

There is a long silence. Suzette is quiet.

Suzette Can we go outside?

Lori Why? Why would we go outside?

Suzette I don't want to talk in here.

Lori Very well.

NINE

Music begins to play. Suzette picks up a coat, which she wraps around her. The two women go out and walk along the street. The lights of London go by. It's romantic.

Suzette I was born in Acton. It was nice because it was full of normal people. Then we all moved up here when Mum became a minister. She said it was nearer to work. Maybe. Technically. By three miles. I don't think there's been a moment in her life when she's taken us into account.

Lori Your mother loves you. She just finds it hard to talk.

Suzette Hey, isn't talking the job?

Lori You said it yourself. There are things beyond words.

They are in Kensington Gardens. They turn round, London on the horizon.

Suzette After a party . . .

Lori Yes?

Suzette One night, I let four men take me.

Lori I'm sorry?

Suzette Didn't you hear what I said?

Lori I heard it but I didn't believe it.

Suzette Well, I did. Most def.

Lori Then I believe you.

Suzette One after the other.

Lori Why did you do that?

Lori waits.

Suzette?

Suzette I was drunk.

She snatches a look at Lori.

Also, everyone keeps telling me, 'Suzette, you're too choosy. You're judgemental. The boys don't like you because they feel judged.'

Lori Who says that?

Suzette Other girls. Afterwards, I lay there thinking, 'Well at least I didn't choose, at least I didn't judge' . . . It was quite peaceful. I could hear them in the next room. I heard one of them say, 'She used to say no to everything. Now she says yes to anything.' Big, big laugh.

She shakes her head, choked up.

It's hard to explain. I was angry. Someone went to the school. They spoke to the headmistress.

Lori When?

Suzette After I was caught smoking dope. Someone had a word.

Lori Was that your mother?

Suzette No.

Lori Who? Who then?

Suzette This man called Otto Fallon.

Lori Otto Fallon?

Suzette Yes.

There's a silence.

Lori He's everywhere, isn't he?

Suzette I was furious. I was going to be expelled, then I wasn't.

Lori Fair enough.

Suzette Yes.

Lori And that's why you slept with four boys. What was it, intense disappointment at not being expelled?

Suzette All right . . .

Lori Come on!

There is a short silence.

Suzette And if you want to know, I'm going to the press.

Lori Oh, are you?

Suzette Like, *yes.*

Lori To say what?

Suzette The school was bought off.

Lori Do you have proof?

Suzette More like suspicion. Matter of fact, this is what I wanted to tell you.

Lori What did you want to tell me?

Suzette I already spoke to a journalist.

There is another short silence.

I told him what happened.

Lori When? When did you speak to a journalist?

Suzette I spoke to a journalist at a party.

Lori What party was that?

Suzette raises her eyebrows.

Just tell me, was he . . .?

Suzette Yes. Yes, as matter of fact he was. He was shagging me.

There's a silence.

Lori Well, this is an interesting moment in all our lives.

Suzette says nothing.

I hope you know what you're doing.

Suzette Is that it? Is that your advice?

Lori It is.

Suzette I thought you were meant to be this brilliant student counsellor. 'I hope you know what you're doing.' It's not life-changing, is it?

Lori smiles in acknowledgement.

Do you think Mum's going to be angry?

Lori You were fucked by four men, and one of them was a journalist – why should she be angry?

Suzette You're right.

Lori Maybe she's looking for a way out of politics. Now she's found it.

Suzette Do you hate me? Do you think worse of me?

Lori I could never hate you.

Suzette Why not?

Suzette moves towards her. Lori puts her arm round her. The glow of the lights has turned orange. Music overwhelms them.

End of Act One.

Act Two

TEN

Music. Monique Toussaint, alone, dressed for a night out and holding a huge martini in a frosted glass.

Monique I don't understand about religion. Do you? I had a Catholic boyfriend. He used to sleep with me, then he'd go to church. I did once say to him, 'As far as I'm concerned, it's fine. You can worship me, then next day you can worship the Virgin Mary.' He replied, 'You don't worship the Virgin Mary, you venerate her.'

The way I look at it is this: if you believe that a woman once gave birth without benefit of intercourse, then you're religious. If you believe that same woman is now eating a cheeseburger and French fries in the room next door, then you're crazy. I have a problem with that.

What worries me, the more sceptical the public becomes, the more devout its leaders. It's like we take the least representative people among us, the only ones who haven't heard the news, and we put them in charge. Now that bothers me.

ELEVEN

Music. A Clerkenwell cocktail bar, called Everest. Motifs of mountains and purity and vodka. Geoff Benzine is nursing a beer. He is handsome, in his thirties, with an expensive haircut. Monique approaches.

Geoff Ah, there you are.

Monique Geoff Benzine?

Geoff Yes.

Monique How are you?

Geoff I'm extremely well.

Monique It's kind of you to meet me.

Geoff Well, I've always wanted to meet you.

Monique I find that very hard to believe. I'm a functionary. I'm a cog.

Geoff Excuse me, but what a cog.

Monique disguises her grimace and sits down.

You got yourself a drink.

Monique Yes.

Geoff I hope you didn't pay for it.

Monique I always prefer to pay for my own.

Geoff It gives you an advantage?

Monique Why would I need an advantage?

Geoff What is it?

Monique It's a triple martini. Just to get me going.

They both smile.

If it's OK with you, we're going to be joined by a friend of mine.

Geoff I thought we were meeting alone.

Monique No. Not alone.

Geoff Foolish of me, I had this wonderful notion we were going to be intimate.

Monique Intimate? No.

Geoff That makes me sad.

Monique How can anyone be intimate with a journalist?

Geoff Well, I can give you the long answer to that question.

Monique Give me the short.

Geoff All right. Remember, the world is full of hypocrites. Everyone pretends to be a nice person, but are they really?

Monique Everyone?

Geoff Well, let's say everyone in public life. Trust me.

Geoff is coming on to her.

Your boss, for instance. Take your boss.

Monique My boss?

Geoff Yes.

Monique What's your problem with Meredith?

Geoff Oh, I'm sure she's pleasant to work for . . .

Monique She is. Extremely.

Geoff Kind to subordinates?

Monique Unfailingly.

Geoff But nobody could look at Meredith's husband and say that he was a model of public probity.

Monique Excuse me, nobody could look at your proprietor.

Geoff No, but the difference is that your boss is elected.

Monique No. The real difference is that your boss is behind bars. He's in the clink, Geoff. Awaiting fraud charges.

Geoff Monique, my proprietor is an innocent victim of this ridiculous public hysteria about corporate governance.

Monique What, and you think politicians can never be innocent victims? Come on, Geoff, you know bloody well.

Geoff What do I know?

Monique Who are you kidding?

Geoff I'm not trying to kid anyone.

Monique Everyone knows. Your employer is a fully-fledged, blue-ribbon, tax-dodging crim. It's a *game*, Geoff.

Geoff Is it?

Monique We all know what your game is. Make life unliveable for politicians.

Geoff Come on, it's a little more complicated than that, isn't it?

Monique You build them up. You knock them down. The press takes up any damn position they fancy – attack from the left one day, attack from the right the next. Don't look for a reason, don't look for a motive. The game is the reason. The game is the motive.

Geoff Hey, and you think *I'm* cynical.

Monique Geoff, press and politicians fight over a very narrow piece of ground. It's because the ground is so narrow that the fight is so intense.

> *Monique is gleaming. Geoff looks at her, half amused, half taken aback.*

Geoff You sound as if you enjoy it.

Monique No. I'm like most people. I take it for what it is.

Geoff Is it what you always wanted? To do this?

Monique As a matter of fact, I was going to be an athlete. I cleared the bar at 1.96 metres. Do you have any idea how high that is?

Geoff Higher than me.

Monique Much. Much higher than you.

Geoff What happened?

Monique I fell. One day at Crystal Palace. In the under-eighteen championships.

Monique looks at him a moment.

I'll tell you what happened, Geoff. I fell at the wrong angle.

Monique gets up as Lori arrives.

And this is my friend.

Lori Monique.

Monique Lori.

They kiss, warmly. Geoff frowns.

Lori I'm sorry if I've kept you waiting.

Monique Lori Drysdale, this is Geoff Benzine.

Lori Well, of course I've read your column . . .

Geoff Thank you.

Lori So I know everything about you.

Monique Well, you would, wouldn't you? After all, that is the principal subject of his column, isn't it? Himself.

The two women smile and sit down. Geoff is discomfited.

But then that's the trend, isn't it? No one's interested any more, are they, in the idea that a newspaper might be there to report the world. No longer happens, does it?

Lori Doesn't seem to.

Monique No, no, the only way you prosper nowadays is by sticking to the endlessly fascinating subject of yourself.

Lori So much easier.

Monique And cheaper, too. None of that expensive business of having to go and get stories.

Lori That's right.

Monique And, let's face it, an added bonus, when journalists write about themselves, then they're finally able to write about people they admire. Gives the whole thing a warmth it might otherwise lack.

Geoff is shifting, uneasy.

Geoff I'm sorry, but I'm just a little bit lost here.

Monique How come?

Geoff For a start, I don't even know what this person does.

Monique 'This person'?

Geoff Yes.

Monique Lori used to be a teacher.

Geoff Ah.

Monique Now she busks.

Geoff She *busks*?

Lori On the District Line.

Geoff And nobody's explained to me what this meeting's about.

Monique flashes her dazzling smile.

Monique Are you going to have a drink?

Lori I'm not. I'm going to watch you.

The complicity between the two women is disturbing Geoff.

Monique I'll tell you what's happening.

Geoff Thank you.

Monique I've been sent here with my friend Lori because we've been tipped off that your paper might be thinking of running a story.

Geoff Oh, really?

Monique Yes.

Geoff What story is that?

Monique I think you know which story it is. Don't you?

Geoff doesn't move a muscle.

Geoff I see. Go on.

Monique We've heard your paper's developing an interest in Otto Fallon.

She holds up a preventative hand.

It's all right. You don't have to say anything.

Geoff I'm not.

Monique Good.

Geoff I'm not saying anything. My paper's always been interested in Otto Fallon. He's done a lot to interest us.

Monique looks at him a moment.

Monique Very well. As you know, Otto is an intensely private man . . .

Geoff I'm not saying anything but I admit I am laughing.

Monique Why are you laughing?

Geoff I'm laughing inside.

Monique Why?

Geoff Why do you think? If he was intensely private, do you really think he'd have run the lottery?

Monique That was some time ago.

Geoff Maybe.

Monique It was a long time ago.

Geoff It's how he made his fortune.

Monique Actually Otto made his fortune in popular music.

Geoff So I suppose he only took over the lottery out of public duty?

Monique smiles.

Monique I don't need to tell you. The lottery distributes large sums of money to deserving causes.

Geoff So it does.

Monique That was Otto's interest.

Geoff Was it?

Monique Certainly.

Geoff That's why he did it? Really? Was that his reason?

Monique Otto welcomed the chance to do what he calls 'put something back'.

Geoff Ah yes.

Monique He loves putting something back. Charity's important to him.

Geoff You don't think the way he got the lottery contract had just a slight smell about it?

Monique As a matter of fact, I don't. You'll remember, there was a parliamentary inquiry into the allocation of that contract.

Geoff There was indeed.

Monique Otto came out with flying colours.

Geoff Yeah. I remember those colours. Shit and shit-brown. If those fly.

Monique He was completely exonerated.

Monique gives him a poker player's stare. She sips her martini.

Geoff All right, but one day somebody's going to explain to me why politicians are drawn to rogues.

Monique Are they?

Geoff I think they are.

Monique Can you generalise like that?

Geoff The interesting thing is, you can.

Monique And if it's true, what do you think it's about?

Geoff Maybe they like the excitement. They like the danger. After all, it's a way of defying the odds, isn't it? Gamblers are drawn to gamblers. People in the limelight want to prove they can get away with it. Specifically there's an erotic pleasure there.

Monique Erotic?

Geoff Yes.

Monique Blimey.

Geoff Yes, that's what gives them a kick. They love to sail close to the wind.

Monique And you, Geoff?

Geoff Me?

Monique Yes.

Geoff Me, what?

Monique My question is: how close do you sail?

Geoff shifts again, his mood changing.

Geoff I'm sorry, I'm not sure I know what this conversation is about. You said you were sent?

Monique Yes.

Geoff Someone sent you? So whose bidding are you doing, Monique?

Monique smiles and looks at Lori.

Monique Look, it's as simple as this. Lori asked to come with me because we're both fans of the column.

Geoff Which column?

Monique Well, that's it. That's my point. You write about parliament, of course you do, you're a sketch-writer, one of the highest paid in Fleet Street.

Geoff I'm not denying it. I've been at the forefront of the battle for journalists' rights.

Monique What rights are those, Geoff? The right to be overpaid?

Geoff nods, acknowledging the joke.

Geoff Look, in case you're wondering, sketch-writing happens to be a great deal harder than it looks.

Monique I'm sure. I never said it was easy.

Geoff Good. Better writers than me have failed at the job.

Monique Little jokes, little quips, always at someone else's expense.

Geoff So? People want newspapers to be fun. I don't see anything wrong with that.

Monique I didn't say it was wrong.

Geoff What would you prefer? That we return to the age of deference? Please.

Monique You may be right.

Geoff I'm sure I am. I don't want to sound pretentious, but you might say mockery oils the wheels of democracy. It's what you might call the essential unguent. Just visit a country that doesn't have a strong, derisive press. See how you like living there. Well?

Monique smiles, insinuating.

Monique But you also do that hackish thing on Saturdays, don't you? You do that column on Saturday.

Geoff Yes, I do.

Monique What's it called?

Geoff You know what it's called. You know perfectly well.

Monique It's true. I do. Lori?

Lori Isn't it called 'The New Man'?

Monique Is that what you are, Geoff? A new man?

Geoff is cold as ice.

You see, Lori and I both love the subject of your Saturday column. It's such an interesting subject, isn't it?

Geoff If you say so.

Monique It's made you pretty well known. I bet people stop you in the street.

Geoff From time to time.

Monique I bet they do.

Geoff The column has a following.

Monique I bet it does. You were the first. When you started. The modern father, the progressive father.

Geoff That's right. That's right. That's the subject.

Monique And we see you on television too.

Geoff So?

Monique Dispensing wisdom, with a self-deprecating air. There you all are, the new men, awash in a bed of nappies and sharing the load with your womenfolk. Oh, it's certainly something, isn't it?

Geoff waits, not knowing where she's going.

And your wife . . .

Geoff What about her? What about my wife? What are you asking?

Neither Monique nor Lori say anything. Geoff looks away, then back, then at his hands. Finally:

And anyway, if you read the column, you would know, she isn't my wife, she's my partner.

Monique But you're close? Certainly as you represent her . . . what a wonderful sense of humour. What a wonderful temperament. What's her name, remind me?

Geoff Her name is Nancy.

Monique Nancy.

Geoff That's her name.

Monique In fact Nancy's the most appealing character in the column. I mean, your children are sweet. How many are there?

Geoff Three.

Monique Darlings. But Nancy's the heart of the thing, don't you think? She always sounds the most understanding of women.

Geoff She is.

Monique And always so forgiving. So forgiving of your behaviour.

Geoff What behaviour? What does she have to forgive?

Monique Oh, you know. The humorous problems you have with the washing machine.

Geoff gets up, furious.

Geoff All right, that's it, I'm out of here. I should never have agreed to meet you.

Monique I'm sorry you feel that.

Geoff As a matter of fact, I do.

Monique It's a shame. Because there are things we'd like to have discussed.

Geoff What things are those? What are they, Monique? Are they to do with rottenness? With rotten government?

Monique Well, if you'd stayed, you would have found out.

Geoff Look, I know what this is! I know what this is about! It's Otto Fallon, isn't it?

Their needling has got to him. Geoff is standing, shouting. Monique is cool.

Monique Geoff, the problem is not what you know, it's how you know it. Now please sit down while Lori talks to you.

Geoff What is Lori going to talk to me about?

Lori The age of consent.

At once Geoff panics, wagging a finger.

Geoff Oh no. No, no, no, this is not going to fly.

Monique Yes. It's going to fly.

Geoff No it's not.

Monique Suzette's age.

Geoff I don't even know who Suzette is. I've never heard of Suzette.

Monique Are you saying you don't know her name?

Geoff I never asked her name!

Monique You never asked it? Sorry, Geoff, run that by me again. You never asked her name? And did you ask her age?

Geoff moves around a little.

Monique Geoff, I think you'd better finish your beer and rearrange your story.

Geoff I don't have a story. Journalists aren't the story!

Monique If only that were true. Do you want another beer?

Geoff No.

Monique Then sit down. This is where Lori comes in.

*Geoff sits. All this time Lori has been sweetly silent.
Now she speaks quietly.*

Lori The thing is this, Geoff, I'm not part of your world.

Geoff I know that.

Lori My interest is not in you. It's in Suzette. Suzette is a girl who did a foolish thing. Most of us have done something similar. At some point. I did. But I was nineteen. That's the difference.

Monique I was twenty-two, my last orgy.

Lori So there you are.

Lori looks at Geoff, level.

Also, I was a professional teacher and my attitude was that children should be allowed to do what they want. I think that stuff about innocence is overrated. Children aren't innocent. And you might argue the sooner they learn about life the better. But I've always felt they should learn about sex from each other, rather than from older men. That does bother me. And it seems also to bother the readers of your family-minded newspaper.

Geoff is completely still.

Monique knows I don't give a damn about Otto Fallon.

Monique It's true. She doesn't.

Lori And, what's more, I don't give a flying fuck for British journalists. Collectively I think you're deluded. You're so callused by arrogance you don't even know you've got a moral problem, let alone the will to do anything about it. You've got 'essential unguents' up the kazoo. However. I do give a damn about Suzette. She's a very brilliant pupil. I don't mean brilliant academically. I mean, she's a brilliant human being.

Lori nods slightly, to let this sink in.

That's why I wanted to come here with Monique.

Geoff Why? Why did you come?

Lori Because I wanted to tell you to fuck off. To your face. In terms you'd never forget.

There's a silence.

Geoff Well, you've done it.

Lori That's right. I've done it.

Geoff I'm not admitting a thing.

Lori Sure.

Geoff I'm not even admitting I know what you're talking about.

Nobody speaks. Finally, reluctantly:

So? What more do you want?

Lori Suzette's a sensitive child and she's going to be a wonderful woman, if she's left alone to work things out for herself. I don't care if bribery was involved in keeping her at school – I don't even know – I really don't. All I care about is her, and her right to live her life with a modicum of dignity. As the rest of us do.

Geoff is nodding now.

Geoff This is blackmail, isn't it?

Lori No.

Monique It's not blackmail.

Lori I don't think you can call it blackmail.

Geoff Why not? Why not blackmail?

Lori Because it's more of a question of behaving in a way which does least harm.

Monique To either of you.

Lori You see, yes, being all over the papers would be bad for Suzette. But also – I'm guessing here, because I've never met Nancy – but I suspect if the full story came out, it might also be bad for you.

When Geoff speaks, he is very controlled.

Geoff Thank you.

Lori Not at all.

Geoff Is that it?

Lori That's it.

Monique That's all.

Lori You've listened to us. You've heard us out.

Geoff Can I say something?

Geoff pauses to gather his thoughts.

In my own case, I wasn't an athlete, I was a scholar.

Lori I'm surprised.

Geoff I was a historian. I did my thesis on trenches and moats.

Lori Really?

Geoff Yes. I'm not being immodest, I'm making a point, but nobody can now write about medieval defences without reference to my work.

Lori Well, that's good.

Geoff I got a first-class degree and I got a doctorate at Oxford. My supervisor said it was the best historical doctorate she'd read in thirty years. I lectured in Nanterre

speaking French and I lectured in Bremen in German.
I don't know how I got into this any more than you do.
A few book reviews. And then.

He shakes his head.

Something's wrong. We all know that. Something's deeply wrong. I can't say if your government is the symptom or if it's the fucking problem. Whichever it is, it's ugly. And that's where I'm leaving it.

Monique This has been very useful.

Geoff It's been useful, yes.

Monique I'll take care of the bill.

Geoff It's yours.

Geoff gets up.

I didn't choose this life. That's my point. I didn't choose it. If I could go back, I would. I wouldn't write those book reviews and I wouldn't become a journalist. But I did. So I can't go back. Goodnight.

Geoff goes out.

Monique What did that mean?

Lori It means we failed.

Monique Yes. That's what I thought.

Lori He's going to go for it.

TWELVE

Meredith, alone.

Meredith This country's under threat. It's under serious threat. I can't tell you the details. I can't tell you where

79

that threat is coming from, or what form it takes. I can only tell you the threat exists. The threat is real.

If you knew the number of dedicated people, enemies, who have been detected and dealt with . . . But of course you don't know, do you? How can you know? Because unfortunately I can't tell you. If I revealed the source of those threats, I'd be giving away intelligence. And that is something I'm not willing to do.

That's why, these days, it's so interesting being a politician. Sorry, but you have to trust us. You have no choice.

THIRTEEN

A rush of music. The sitting room of a Westminster apartment. Big sofas, chintz, the floor strewn with children's toys. Meredith comes in to greet Alec Beasley. He is tall, good-looking, in his forties, toned by squash, in blue jeans and sweatshirt.

Alec Meredith.

Meredith Alec, good evening, I do apologise.

Alec No need.

Meredith Encroaching like this.

Alec makes a courteous nod, acknowledging.

Alec The usual thing is to say, 'One gets so little time.' But is it true?

Meredith I don't know. You tell me.

Alec In fact, funny thing, I was saying to my team the other day, I'm not actually that busy.

Meredith Really?

Alec I played golf earlier.

Meredith Excellent.

Alec I put the kids to bed.

Alec smiles, at ease.

After a year or two, I suddenly caught myself drumming my fingers. I had this job under my belt, more or less.

Meredith That quick?

Alec Of course one can never say entirely.

Meredith Of course not.

Alec There's always the unexpected.

Meredith Yes there is.

Alec On the other hand, after a while, one does begin to recognise patterns. Familiar patterns, familiar solutions. Understand, I'm not saying I'm bored. I'm not.

Meredith I'm sure you're not. How could you be?

Alec But it's like anything. Always more rewarding when you're learning, isn't it?

Meredith And now?

Alec Now? Well now, one almost craves a crisis.

Alec is stretching back, arms wide, on the sofa.

Of course, it's different for you, isn't it, Meredith?

Meredith In a way, yes.

Alec Your department is different. In the Home Office. Life is an endless succession of crises. One damn thing after another, eh?

Meredith waits, not reacting.

81

But also, Meredith, if I can say this, you have a different temperament from me. You have a different investment.

Meredith Do you think so?

Alec You love politics. For what it is. I don't. I love it only for what I can get done.

Meredith I've heard you say that before.

Alec I'm sure you have.

Meredith You say that often.

Alec That's quite possible. Any politician who has a horror of repetition hasn't got the hang of the thing at all.

He smiles, benign.

But you see, the difference between us, Meredith, is that I could walk away. I could walk away tomorrow and still be happy. I wouldn't miss it.

Meredith Wouldn't you?

Alec No, I wouldn't.

Meredith Are you thinking of walking away?

Alec No, Meredith, I'm not. As a matter of fact, I'm thinking of staying.

Alec has shown sudden steel. A moment, then the charm returns.

Only for a time, mark you. I've never regarded being Prime Minister as the be-all and end-all.

Meredith You've made that plain.

Alec There are far more interesting things to do in life.

Meredith I know you think that.

Alec Please, don't mistake me – it's an honour, it's an

honour to serve. I love the job. But nevertheless, one comes to feel one might like to leave at the moment of one's own choosing.

Alec smiles, a touch dangerous.

Do you know that expression, 'That which doesn't kill you makes you stronger'?

Meredith I've heard it, yes.

Alec I've never understood it. I was thinking about it in church this morning. Surely that which doesn't kill you makes you weaker, doesn't it? I would have thought.

Meredith I'm not sure.

Alec How can it make you stronger? After all, how much punishment can one person take? And what good does it do them? In fact, speaking from experience, I'd say survival is largely about dodging the blows . . .

Meredith Indeed.

Alec Avoiding the blows, not walking into them. Hmm? And in the last few weeks I can't help noticing we seem to have been taking quite a few. Both of us.

Meredith I assumed that's why you wanted to talk to me.

Alec looks at her a moment.

Alec I've met your youngest, haven't I?

Meredith She had a birthday party, remember?

Alec Of course I remember.

Meredith When she was ten.

Alec That's right.

Meredith You made her incredibly happy.

Alec Did I really?

Meredith She talked about it for years. 'The Prime Minister came to my party.' You brought her a cake. A cake with pink icing.

Alec Lovely girl. Where is she now?

Meredith She's in hiding.

Alec Left the country?

Meredith nods.

Well, that's sensible.

Meredith It seemed important.

Alec I don't need to know where.

Meredith I'm not going to tell you where.

Alec But you know?

Meredith nods again.

Somewhere beyond the long lens.

Meredith just looks.

Nowhere East, I hope.

Meredith No, not East.

Alec Good.

Meredith South.

Alec Excellent. Towards the sun. She'll come out of all this as brown as a Bedouin.

He smiles at the thought.

Of course – it's hard, isn't it? When it's family?

Meredith It certainly is.

Alec It's worse when it's family.

Meredith That's what I've been wanting to discuss with you. But it's been hard to get to see you. I can't even get you on the phone.

But Alec goes on, ignoring this.

Alec As for oneself, one's used to a certain level of scrutiny . . .

Meredith Of course.

Alec Very early on, one becomes immune. But when a child is involved. I've been thinking so much about you.

Meredith It's been a low point. The lowest. I don't mean professionally.

Alec Of course not.

Meredith I mean personally.

Alec Of course.

Meredith With Suzette.

Alec It's at this moment, isn't it? Isn't this the moment, Meredith, when you ask, when you have to ask yourself, 'Is this worth it? Is this worth the price?'

A decisive moment has been reached. Neither of them moves. Meredith is cautious.

Meredith I've asked that question.

Alec Have you?

Meredith Yes. Yes. Inevitably.

Alec I'm sure.

Meredith These last few weeks.

Alec You've asked it?

Meredith Yes. In the middle of the night. I've been alone in the middle of the night.

Alec Jack not there?

Meredith No.

Alec Jack not with you?

Meredith No.

There is a charged silence.

Alec I don't want to make this conversation too formal, Meredith. I want to keep it fluid.

Meredith You're keeping it fluid.

Alec I'm certainly trying.

Meredith You're succeeding.

Alec I want us both to leave the room satisfied with what we've decided.

Meredith I want that too.

Alec I want us at peace. Not just with each other but also at peace with ourselves.

He smiles, easing up.

After all, I don't forget, you were my campaign manager.

Meredith A long time ago.

Alec When I went for the leadership. We've come a long way. You and I.

Meredith It was a wonderful time.

Alec It certainly was.

Meredith It was the best time.

There is a sensual silence.

Alec Nobody thought I would make it. I sometimes look back and think: who believed in me? Who really believed?

Meredith Honestly, it wasn't very difficult.

Alec You say that now.

Meredith It was pretty obvious you were going to be leader. The only question was when.

Alec Committing to me early needed courage. It needed foresight. You had that courage. You had that foresight. They were great days.

Meredith Yes. Yes they were.

Both of them are thinking those days over. It's intimate. Meredith speaks quietly, taking a risk.

Can I say something you're not going to like?

Alec Please. Say anything.

Meredith It's never been the same since Otto arrived.

Alec is completely still.

Alec Ah.

Meredith Oh, I know why you need him, I know your reasons.

Alec I hope you do.

Meredith They're clear. But everyone feels – all your colleagues feel – we've never been as close since Otto.

Alec That may be true.

Meredith You used to summon us in – I don't know – for late nights like this. So many late nights – even when you first moved to Downing Street . . .

Alec Yes.

Meredith It was open house. Your children running around. Pizza. You saying, 'Oh, let's open a bottle.' And now? Well, now we never see you. 'Anyone seen Alec?' 'Oh, Alec's gone up to Hampstead to be with Otto.'

Alec It is work, you know.

Meredith I know.

Alec I do go there to work.

Meredith I know.

Alec Who do you think pays for the Labour Party?

He shrugs.

I have to go. It's a duty. I go to raise money, I go to raise funds . . .

Meredith But you like it too.

Alec Are you saying I've changed?

Meredith Of course. Of course you've changed. Don't you think so?

Alec Maybe.

Meredith You wouldn't be human if you hadn't.

Alec And not for the better, is that it?

Meredith You're tougher.

Alec smiles, modest.

Alec I like Otto, it's true. I like his company. Other people come to me and ask things of me. He asks nothing. In a funny way, for a man who combs his hair backwards, he has no vanity.

Meredith Are you sure?

Alec I know him inside out.

Meredith But it's him that got us into this mess.

Alec Did he?

Meredith Certainly he did.

Alec That may be a matter of opinion.

Meredith Is it?

Alec I think it is.

Meredith It was Otto's doing. The whole thing was Otto's fault. I'm sorry, but it's impossible to see it any other way.

Alec From your perspective.

Meredith No. Not from my perspective. From any perspective.

Alec How so?

Meredith He's a governor of the school. For goodness' sake, it was him that made the offer.

Alec He did make the offer, yes.

Meredith A new school gym. That's what he offered.

Alec So it appears.

Meredith He did it! It was his decision. He never even spoke to me.

Alec No one has suggested he did.

Meredith Well, actually they have. The papers have.

Alec Oh, the papers!

He shrugs, as if the press were absurd.

Meredith That's what they want. That's what they're looking for. The smoking gun. The direct connection that links me to the bribe.

Alec But they haven't found it, have they?

Meredith Of course they haven't. They haven't found it because it doesn't exist.

Alec You didn't know? You knew nothing? What did you know?

Meredith I've told you. I knew nothing. For God's sake, I didn't even know Otto was on the board of governors.

Alec Didn't you?

Meredith No. No, I didn't.

Alec Nobody told you?

He pauses, apparently casual.

Nobody showed you a prospectus? You didn't see a prospectus?

Meredith looks, calculating.

Meredith What I'm saying is, look at the way he handled it, Alec. Twenty-four hours after Suzette was caught smoking dope, Otto endowed the school with a new gym. You don't think that was just a little bit gauche?

Alec A little bit.

Meredith A little bit obvious? What I find incredible: the guy's meant to be experienced. He's meant to be some sort of brilliant manipulator. Don't you think he could have tried to be just a little bit more subtle?

Alec Well, that's Otto, isn't it?

Meredith Is that all you can say? 'That's Otto'?

Alec Otto was doing what he thought was right.

Meredith Yes, but it wasn't, was it?

Alec He was trying to help.

Meredith has raised her voice.

Come on, now, Meredith . . .

Meredith Come on what?

Alec You know this is painful for me. A series of things have happened –

Meredith They certainly have.

Alec – none of which could have been predicted, none of which could have been prepared for. The fact is, we've had a run of bad luck.

Meredith To put it no higher.

Alec Some debauched journalist, some lecher, without the slightest regard for his own self-interest, decides to go ahead and run a story, even if the details of how he got it may entail the destruction of his own career. A self-loathing medievalist, who hates himself and everyone else.

Meredith Well, in his case there's plenty to loathe.

Alec Indeed.

Meredith More than plenty.

Alec What can you do? This is a man who seems willing to lose reputation if it means he gains fame.

Meredith Yes, well, that's an exchange a lot of journalists are willing to make.

Alec And not just journalists.

They are snapping at each other.

Honestly, be fair, Meredith, how could anyone prepare for that?

Meredith And Benzine hasn't destroyed his career. He's been sacked by one paper, that's all.

Alec All right.

Meredith For admitting to sex with the Home Secretary's daughter. Whereupon he's been eagerly taken on by another.

Alec I did see that.

Meredith To write his story!

Alec I agree. Deplorable.

Meredith On the grounds that she was sixteen. Sixteen! By six weeks. This man can make a killing, he's trampling all over the Press Complaints Commission because, by a bat squeak, Suzette was no longer fifteen. And they lecture us, they lecture *us* about ethics . . .

Alec However.

He tries to focus Meredith's anger.

Alec I know, I do know what you've been through, Meredith . . .

Meredith It's been hell.

Alec We do have to look at the context. All this would be fine, everything that's happening now would be fine, we could live through it, if you didn't come to us, Meredith, with – how do I put it? – your garments already stained.

Meredith looks down, conceding.

Meredith I know.

Alec I'm just saying.

Meredith It's a problem. I know it's a problem.

Alec You're running out of Teflon, Meredith. Unlucky things happen to unlucky people.

There's a silence.

Well?

Meredith Alec, I've been thinking about this.

Alec I hope you have.

Meredith Day after day. I think of little else.

Alec And?

Meredith I want this to work out for everyone.

Alec That's what I want.

Meredith And I do mean everyone.

Alec gestures for her to go ahead.

I know you have mixed feelings about Jack. You always have. I understand that. Sometimes for the government he represents quite an embarrassment. However. I've made a decision.

Alec What decision is that?

Meredith I'm going to stand by him.

Alec I see.

Meredith Whatever.

Alec What does that mean? Does that mean you're willing to resign?

Meredith gives him a stare which means 'No'. Alec moves a little round the room.

I'm trying to take in the nuances here, Meredith.

Meredith I'm sure you are.

Alec God knows, a prime minister is hardly a trained psychiatrist, but on occasions I have been forced to wonder – forgive me – I've found myself wondering just how close your marriage is.

Meredith shifts.

Meredith Look, if you're asking –

Alec I think you know what I'm asking.

Meredith Then in that case, yes, you're right. It's been wretched between us for a long time. I'm not going to go into detail but it's been a very long time since Jack and I were intimate.

Alec I understand.

Meredith A very long time. He was probably wearing flares. You know Jack . . .

Alec I've known him since he was a student.

Meredith Exactly. And so have I. At the best of times, Jack is a forceful man with strong and complicated needs.

Alec Indeed.

Meredith Those needs can become exhausting. Over the years.

Alec Jack and Meredith. Meredith and Jack. For as long as I can remember.

Meredith Quite.

Alec You were childhood sweethearts.

There is a moment's silence.

Meredith Alec, I've never known anyone else.

Alec is taken aback.

My whole life. I've known him since he was sixteen. And he was the best-looking boy in the class.

Alec Still is.

Meredith However, I do have to face the prospect of my husband making a series of court appearances. He's scheduled to appear in a number of trials.

Alec I've heard of three.

Meredith I don't want to go through Jack's whole investment history . . .

Alec No need.

Meredith It's been pretty innovative. As markets have turned down, so entrepreneurs have had to become more ingenious. Go East and inevitably countries become more volatile. All right, I'm not going to question my husband's integrity –

Alec Please don't.

Meredith – but I can give my opinion of his judgement.

Alec He's been a bloody fool.

Meredith Exactly.

Alec Worse than a fool! And for a Labour government, it's hard to sustain the prolonged prospect of the Home Secretary's husband appearing in the dock, in handcuffs, in countries where they don't speak English.

Meredith Yes. Yes, I can see that's bothering for you.

Alec is thoughtful.

So?

Alec I'm going to be frank with you, Meredith.

Mcredith I would expect nothing less.

Alec If your choice is to remain in office, then – I've spoken to my team, and they recommend you put some distance between yourself and your husband.

Meredith Distance?

Alec Yes.

Meredith What sort of distance do you have in mind?

Alec looks at her a moment.

Alec Again, believe me, I would never dare to stray into an area where my advice was unwanted . . .

Meredith It's wanted.

Alec There's a line here and it mustn't be crossed.

Meredith Cross it.

Alec But if your marriage is indeed, as you represent it, extinct, I suppose I'm wondering if you could find some more public means of expressing that extinction.

There's a short silence.

Meredith I see.

Alec Yes.

Meredith I see.

Alec Yes. I'm proposing this for your own benefit.

Meredith I'm sure you are.

Alec Why suffer a burden you don't need to carry?
A simple gesture at this stage.

Meredith Divorce Jack?

Alec Not necessarily.

Meredith A separation? A trial separation? What, a *period* of separation?

Alec looks, unwilling to be specific.

Alec Meredith, as you know, my religious beliefs run deep, they run very deep, I would never ask anyone to do anything against the promptings of their own conscience. We're moving into uncharted waters. We're already in the middle of a storm and the forecast is worse. It's not up to me to advance a specific prescription.

Meredith You mean I might get a divorce and still lose my job?

She has spoken sharply. Now Alec takes her on.

Alec Meredith, I hope you understand the spirit in which this is being suggested.

Meredith I understand that spirit.

Alec You're hardly in a position to demand guarantees.

Alec has been forceful. He waits.

Well?

Meredith gets up, moves across the room, then turns, decisive.

Meredith There are these moments, aren't there? There are these moments.

Alec You tell me.

Meredith This is what you prepare for. The moments when you have to show there's more to politics than making speeches and pretending to like football.

She is implacable.

I first saw Jack across a classroom in Wolverhampton. He was sixteen. He had ink on his fingers, and a dirty laugh. I loved that laugh. I still do. We've been married for twenty-four years. Yes, you may say that marriage is not everything either of us might wish it to be. But it's ours.

It's what we have left. Again, you may say it's unwise for me to stand by a man who has so many obvious flaws. But I wonder if someone who's blindly loyal to Otto Fallon is in the best position to make that judgement.

The two stare at each other.

Alec All right, good, very well, I see.

Meredith I'm going to survive, Alec.

Alec If you say so.

Meredith And so is Suzette. And so is Jack. We're going to come through. What, I get hounded from office by the British press?

Alec Of course not.

Meredith We all started together fifteen years ago and who's left?

Alec Very few.

Meredith I've watched too many good people go down. Remember, Alec, the British like a battler.

Alec They do. It's true.

Meredith They do.

Alec They like a battler, yes. Understandably they're less keen on psychopaths.

Meredith Maybe. But in our profession it's a fine line, Alec. You know that.

She has stood up. She is formal.

If you want to get rid of me, you're going to have to sack me.

Alec I see.

Meredith I won't go quietly. Alec, I won't.

She looks at him, unrelenting.

My husband is facing a series of unwarranted charges which have nothing to do with my political career. My daughter is therefore experiencing a period of personal turbulence during which we ask her privacy to be respected. How does that sound?

Alec Impregnable.

Meredith That's what we're saying then.

She nods, still formal.

Thank you for seeing me.

Alec Not at all.

Meredith smiles, about to go.

Meredith One thing, Prime Minister: what's happening with the gym?

Alec The gym?

Meredith Yes.

Alec What should be happening? Naturally, the gym is going ahead.

Meredith Is it?

Alec Why wouldn't it? For the gym not to go ahead would be effectively an admission of guilt. And that is something Otto is not prepared to make.

Meredith You've spoken to him?

Alec doesn't answer.

Alec, why does Otto mean more to you than the government?

FOURTEEN

Frank, alone, in a dinner suit.

Frank I did once sleep with a woman. I did. Once. It was nice enough, but it was non-addictive. I don't think men like it really, do they? Oh, they pretend they do. But they'd rather sleep with each other. There's something reassuring, isn't there, about sleeping with someone who isn't that much different from you?

I'm not saying all MPs are gay, they're not, but let's say someone like me goes to Westminster, they don't exactly feel they have to show their passport.

Otto and I were called in to help the Minister for Defence Procurement who sustained mysterious injuries one night on Hampstead Heath. He was walking the dog. Only problem was, he didn't have a dog. Otto looked at me – that look of his. 'Get the man a dog.' I went down to Battersea, got him a mutt. He loves that mutt, he's still got it. His kids love that mutt. And he's still an MP.

FIFTEEN

A rush of music. The kitchen of Otto's home, architect-designed. Doors lead off into the main area. Frank is fussing over some plates of food as Mike hovers.

Mike Do you think he'll see me?

Frank Of course he'll see you, he always does, why wouldn't he?

Mike Then why've I been waiting so long? I've been trying to see him for days.

Frank You seem in a state.

Mike I am in a state.

Frank It's nothing to worry about. I know for a fact: you're a favourite of his. He holds you in high esteem, Mike. He's got great plans for you.

Mike shifts.

Mike I don't know. Maybe it's . . .

Frank What?

Mike No maybe it's just . . . with the Prime Minister coming.

Frank Oh, sure. The Prime Minister.

Otto appears, also in evening dress, shirt cuffs flowing from the ends of his sleeves. He is in very good spirits.

Otto All right everybody, tell me what you think. What do you think of me?

Frank You look great.

Otto Mike?

Mike Fine.

Otto Here I am, dressed up for a hog-killing. Tell me honestly: would I pass at a posh do?

Frank This is a posh do.

Otto Every time I pull on a dinner jacket, I ask myself the question, 'Now who exactly is fooling who?'

Frank It's a good question.

Otto It's interesting, Frank always says high society is driven by fear.

Frank It's true. Pure fear.

Otto They all think the same, they all dress the same, they eat in the same restaurants . . .

Frank They eat in your restaurant.

Otto There can only be one reason: they're all frightened!

Otto has raised his voice in mock-terror. Frank smiles to himself, fiddling with the food.

There's more independence of thought in the Finchley Rotary Club than there is in the British establishment.

Frank It's just a dinner jacket, Otto.

Otto Maybe.

Mike I've been wondering, Otto, it is quite urgent, I need to have a word with you.

But Otto has sat down to deal with an obstinate cufflink.

Otto I tell you, Mike, the cleverest thing you can do is to see it all as history.

Frank What do you know about history?

Otto As it happens, you ginger oaf, I know quite a lot. One thing I know: periods of extreme licence are always followed by periods of extreme discipline.

Frank Is this what you call a period of licence?

Otto There's always a reaction.

Frank Is that so?

Otto Once the bonds break, once the ties begin to fray, once people start smoking dope and walking naked into the woods, you can be pretty sure the Nazis won't be far behind. What I'm saying is, Mike, enjoy your freedom while you may because you can be damn sure it won't last for ever.

Frank turns, amused.

Frank I don't know what's happening. My boss seems to be turning philosophical.

Otto I am philosophical.

Frank His new position seems to have gone to his head.

Otto You're just jealous. Sorry, Frank, not everyone can be Chairman of Covent Garden. Right at the heart, right at the plump mucky heart of the thing. Imagine.

Frank Imagine.

Otto Well, it is something. Come on, a boy from North London . . .

Frank Oh God, *déjà vu*. Show us your roots, Otto.

Otto Me, of all people, put in charge of the mood music of the ruling class.

He rubs his hands, delighted.

I'll tell you what I said.

Frank When?

Otto When they approached me, when they sounded me out.

Frank What did you say?

Otto I said I'm happy to do the job. Royal Opera House? I can do that. Just as long as I don't have to step inside the auditorium.

Frank God forbid.

Otto No thank you. I'll stay outside in the bar, practising my grin and emptying people's pockets.

Otto turns back to Mike, nostalgic.

Have I ever told you, Mike, have I ever told you this?

Mike I don't know. I don't know till you tell me.

Otto Well, this is it. I made my fortune with just three chords.

Frank It's true. He did.

Otto I'd been slaving in Tin Pan Alley, pushing out one record after another, I'd actually been doing it for a while, then when I had a hit I thought, 'Hang on,' I thought, 'I've heard those chords before.'

Frank That's when he realised. It's a formula.

Otto Find some young lads, working-class lads, put them in kilts or tight trousers, play those chords.

Frank Da-da-da. In that order.

Otto Years later somebody explained to me, a musicologist explained to me, they're called aspirational eighths.

Frank They're anthemic.

Otto That's right. 'Anthemic.' Nobody understands why, but play those chords and people feel hope.

Mike Is it really that simple? You think you can take people for fools?

For the first time Otto takes Mike in.

Otto I don't know, Mike. You've worked here long enough. Do you think that's what we do? Take people for fools?

Mike looks straight at him.

Mike Well, you must admit, you do have the most extraordinary confidence.

Otto People want to feel hope. Da-da-da. It's an animal thing.

Mike Yes, but for example, if you look at tonight, if you just look at it, objectively you do seem very certain.

Otto Certain of what?

Mike You seem so convinced that people are still going to come.

Otto Why wouldn't they come?

Mike For the obvious reasons.

Otto Which are?

Mike It's one thing to be associated with a political party when they're on the way up. But when they're on the way down . . .

Otto Are we on the way down?

He throws up a hand.

No, I'm kidding.

Mike The government plummeting in the polls – fifteen points behind one day, twenty points the next.

Otto And that bothers you, does it, Mike?

Mike I'm just saying: things being as they are. For a start, I'd be interested to know, what's the Prime Minister feeling?

Otto What's he feeling?

Mike Yes.

Otto Feeling? Alec?

Mike Yes.

Otto I don't think Alec's feeling too bad. What do you think, Frank? Have you seen him lately?

Frank I saw him yesterday. He seemed OK. He's got a Home Secretary he can't rid of. Otherwise . . .

Mike I don't understand. It's a crisis. People are talking as if the government could fall.

Otto Well?

He smiles at Mike.

And?

Otto has tied his shoelaces. Now he gets up.

Mike, there's one thing you do have to understand about Alec.

Mike What's that?

Otto Alec's always seen Downing Street as sort of a stepping stone.

Mike A stepping stone?

Otto Yes.

Mike A stepping stone to what?

Otto Oh, you know.

Mike No, I don't know.

Otto Bigger things.

Otto smiles at Frank, who smiles back.

I mean, it's a small kind of mind, isn't it, that cares about any kind of position. Once you start caring about positions, you're dead. 'Oh, I'm Prime Minister. Wow!' No, if you're serious, you're always on your way, aren't you? You're on the way to somewhere else. Isn't that what it's about?

Mike Is it?

Otto I think so, Mike. Apart from anything – look, I'm just guessing – but I imagine Alec would quite like to be rich.

The door opens and Meredith comes in with Monique, both dressed up.

Meredith Otto, you rogue, you're hiding from your own party.

Otto Meredith. And from what I've heard, so are you.

They kiss.

What a pleasure.

Meredith It's mutual.

Otto I had no idea you were intending to honour us.

Meredith Nor did I. I haven't been out in weeks. I was getting tired of my own company. So I thought I might go out on the town.

Otto See what happens.

Meredith Exactly.

Otto Show yourself.

Meredith And what better occasion than your new appointment? Congratulations, Otto. I had no idea you liked opera.

Otto I love it.

Frank I'll get us some canapés. And something to drink.

He goes out.

Meredith I don't believe you've met my special adviser?

Otto Have we met?

Meredith No, you haven't. Or if you have, I most certainly didn't know about it.

Otto In that case: how do you do?

Monique No. How do *you* do?

They shake hands.

Otto I didn't catch your name.

Monique Monique. And I'm guessing but you must be . . .

Otto Otto Fallon. I raise money for the party.

Monique It's a pleasure.

Otto And by the way, this is Mike. Do you know Mike Drysdale?

Mike Minister.

Meredith hesitates. They shake hands.

Meredith Of course I know Mike. You used be at the Home Office.

Mike Yes.

Meredith And if I'm right, I think it's your wife . . .

Mike It is.

Meredith Even now. Have you spoken to her?

Mike Yes, I have. I speak to her every day.

Meredith She's with my daughter?

Mike She is.

Meredith They're together?

Mike Yes. In fact that's what I'm doing here. I've been trying to talk to Otto.

Meredith You work for Otto now?

Mike I do.

Meredith That must be rewarding.

Mike Sometimes. But there are times when Otto can be hard to get hold of. He has methods. He has techniques.

Mike has raised his voice, hardened his tone.

Otto Look, perhaps we should leave this for another occasion. It sounds as if Mike's looking to pick a bone with me.

Meredith Mike seems to be implying he's unhappy in his work.

Otto That's exactly what he's implying.

Meredith I'd love to know why. How can anyone not be happy working for Otto?

Otto looks a moment, then waves a hand.

Otto Very well. It doesn't bother me. If that's what you want, please go ahead, speak in front of the minister.

He smiles. Meredith waits.

Mike All right. All right, if you want to know, if you want the truth, I'm feeling it's time for me to resign. In fact that's what I'm doing. I'm offering my resignation. Here. Right now. In the kitchen.

Otto I see.

He looks at Mike a moment.

Are you going to tell me why?

Mike Lots of reasons.

Otto Give me one.

Mike Well, if you really want me to say –

Otto It was you that jumped in, Mike. Now, please, pull yourself out.

Mike All right: for some time now, I've been finding my work pretty tricky.

Otto Tricky? How? In what way?

Mike I don't think I've quite got the hang of it. I mean I'm not incompetent, I have worked out a spiel, I have a spiel . . . it isn't difficult . . .

Otto I'm sure.

Mike I hear this rubbish pouring out of me, it comes out of me, I have no idea where from: I talk to the clients, I talk to the donors, I give them a speech about stepping up to the plate, taking responsibility, doing one's share, *taking part.*

Otto So? Why is that rubbish?

Mike I stand there, I say to them, 'You're bankers, you're businessmen, you know as well as me, democracy can't function unless people are committed to its organisations. And, after all, these organisations have to be paid for. They don't pay for themselves.'

Otto Quite right. So?

Mike And then they usually say, 'Yes, I see, well I'd be very happy to help, I'm a big fan of Alec,' they say. 'Remarkable man,' they say. 'Not like the usual socialist.'

Otto But?

He waits.

But?

Mike But then I grind to a halt, because frankly I have a problem.

Otto What problem is that?

Mike Forgive me. I see what they're giving us. They're giving us money. But I'm still unclear what we're giving them.

Otto I see. Yes. Yes. And this question troubles you?

Mike looks straight at him.

Mike It's not just this question.

Otto Other questions?

Mike I'm sorry, I've no wish to be offensive. I suppose I've been shocked lately, I've been a little shocked.

Meredith By what?

Mike By you.

Meredith I've shocked you?

Mike Yes.

Meredith How have I shocked you, then?

She is poker-faced.

Mike I don't know, it's none of my business, but I saw quite a lot of Suzette before she went abroad, in fact you might say Suzette was more at our house than she was at yours. She was with Lori a lot of the time, most of the time. And now, well, now you seem to spend all your time defending your husband. On the airwaves. In the papers. Maybe that's right. I don't know. But we were with a girl who was crying out for her parents. And, what's worse, what seems worse to me, nobody seems shocked. Nobody's surprised by your priorities. The episode's disturbed me. It disturbed me profoundly. Because I've begun to think, what is this? What's going on? Who are we?

Otto 'Who are we?'

Mike Yes.

Otto In what sense? In what sense, who are we?

There is a moment of incomprehension.

It doesn't affect *you*, does it?

Mike Well, in some funny way, I feel it does. I've begun to feel I've woken up in a foreign country. As if everyone held a meeting and I wasn't invited. A motion was passed, something rather important was decided, but I'm the only person who hasn't been told. Sometimes I think, is this what going mad is like?

Mike stops a moment.

Mike OK, for one reason or another the government's in trouble, the papers are after Meredith, they'd love to destroy her . . .

Monique They certainly would.

Mike Just as they'd love to destroy the Prime Minister –

Meredith Oh yeah, throw *him* in and make stew –

Mike And meanwhile, forgive me, but there's a general sense of weirdness – wars which last for ever and are going nowhere, and policies which are nothing but rhetoric, they're just rhetoric – they bear no relation to the facts – but even so.

Otto Even so?

Mike looks at Meredith.

Mike You're still in office.

Otto Mike, she's committed no crime.

Mike stares a moment.

Mike So I suppose what I'm really saying is this: I've reserved a ticket. I'm going to Sicily. That's where they are. Am I allowed to say that?

Meredith By all means.

Mike In a hotel by the sea. I'm leaving in the morning. That's why it was urgent.

Meredith You're joining Suzette?

Mike The way I'd put it is: I'm joining Lori. I've never been through anything like this. I'm feeling if I don't join Lori, I'm going to go out of my head.

Mike is distraught, but before anyone can react Frank comes back in.

Frank What I've done is, I've taken a very thin slice of Spanish ham and I've just *drizzled* on some virgin olive oil, it's a first pressing – well, I'm not going to bore you with the provenance, but let's just say you're going to taste it and then you're going to die.

Otto Frank, you may have to hold off for a moment.

Frank Nobody's hungry?

Otto Worse than that. We're confronting some charges which Mike has put to us.

Mike I haven't put any charges. I'm just uncomfortable.

Otto Are you? Is it you who's uncomfortable, Mike? Or tell me, is it your wife?

He turns to Frank.

Frank, I'm putting you in charge. We're going to pay Mike off. Whatever he wants. We're going to give him a big cheque and we're going to buy him a ticket to Sicily.

Mike No, really.

Otto I insist. It's the least we can do. In a moment we all have to go to a party, and we have to go in good spirits. I want everyone happy. It bores me when people aren't. The point is this, Mike: I've met your wife, she came here once, remember? We had a good talk, she's smart as a whip and I was left with the feeling she doesn't altogether approve of what we do.

Mike She's never said that.

Otto No, of course not. But my guess is you're leaving your job to try and please her. Am I right?

He waits.

Am I right?

Mike In a way. Partly. Yes, you're right. That's part of it.

Otto I thought so.

Mike OK!

Mike has shouted. Now everyone is staring at him.

Otto You're scared of your wife, Mike?

Mike No. No, of course not. But I'm scared of losing her.

Otto Then you will.

Mike looks appalled. It's very quiet.

There's no question, you must leave in the morning.

Mike Thank you.

Otto Frank, you'll see to it?

Frank Sure.

Mike Thank you. Thank you very much.

Otto Now you have what you want.

Mike turns to Meredith.

Mike You probably don't know. Lori chose the hotel because it's where we went on our honeymoon. It's right by the sea. The press would never think of it, that's one thing. But also she wanted to go back where we'd been happiest.

There is a silence, everyone a little shaken.

Frank Otto, I'm sorry, but the guests are getting restless. They need you to make an appearance.

Otto I'll make an appearance. We're winding up here.

Mike I think we are.

Meredith shakes Mike's hand.

Meredith It was nice to see you again. If I can say a word . . .?

Mike Please do.

Meredith If I may say this: you worry about things which don't matter. Truly. Your wife matters. She's a remarkable woman.

Mike I think so too.

Meredith Worry about her. She's worth worrying about. On the other hand, I don't think you should worry too much about what the donors get back. They know what they're getting.

Mike What do they get?

Meredith They get low tax. It isn't said, but that's what they get. A business-friendly environment. That means low tax. Put it another way: they give money to keep their money.

Mike I see.

Meredith Yes.

Mike It's as simple as that.

Meredith And as to the rest, I'm sorry to have shocked you, but I'm afraid it's necessary. The saddest thing about politics: the bodies of the fallen soldiers, scattered by the roadside. The saddest thing. So forgive me, I made a resolution. Rightly or wrongly, but I made it. I came home one night, I sat alone one night, in my darkened living room – a long night of the soul – and I decided not to be one of those bodies. Not to fall by the roadside. And that is it.

She is quite still.

Once they hated us because we were socialists. Now they hate us because we're not. I've discovered a curious kind of freedom. Because whatever you do, they're going to dislike it. So you might as well do what you want.

They are all still a moment, suspended.

Otto Da-da-da.

Meredith So.

Otto Good. Real feelings.

Meredith All right. This is a lovely party, Otto. I'm enjoying it to the full.

Otto So am I.

Meredith I'm already meeting interesting people. Now, what are my orders? Who do you want me to talk to? Lead me to them. And I want to see Alec. I haven't seen Alec in weeks.

The group has moved to the door. Frank opens it. Otto has taken her arm.

Otto Keep going, Meredith.

Meredith I will.

Otto There's only one crime, and that's giving up.

Meredith Monique?

Monique Yes?

Meredith Murmur the names.

They sweep out in a hail of 'Hello, how are you?'
The door closes. Frank is left in the room with Mike.
He returns to gather up more food.

Mike How long will it last?

Frank A couple of hours.

Mike I don't mean the party.

Frank Oh.

Frank thinks a moment.

It'll last while the money lasts.

There is a shared moment between them. Then music
begins to play and Frank goes.

SIXTEEN

Suzette alone, in improvised summer clothing.

Suzette He fancies me. I know he does. I know he fancies
me. This skinny boy at the beach. He'd die rather than
show it. You don't show it, do you? If you show it, you
lose status. He never looks at me, and I never look at him.
We've never spoken. But we're on.

There are certain clues. Like how we're physically
compatible. I would just fit in the crook of his arm. He's
noticed that.

I have heard his voice. One day he was walking past
me, I turned over on my towel just as he went by – my

body was sizzling with oil, I was like a grilled sardine, feeling lovely, looking lovely – and I heard him say to his friend, 'I wouldn't shag that if it was the last hole on earth.' I think that's pretty conclusive, don't you?

SEVENTEEN

A swell of music. The terrace of the small hotel gives out onto the blue Sicilian sea. Lori and Suzette are sitting at a table, empty glasses beside them.

Suzette So he's not coming.

Lori No. No. He wanted to come. He had a ticket.

Suzette So what happened?

Lori I asked him not to.

Suzette What did you say to him?

Lori I told him I wasn't ready. I told him I needed time.

Suzette Did you say you needed space?

Lori I didn't use that phrase, no.

Suzette You sound like one of those women in novels about old people.

Lori 'Old' meaning?

Suzette Over thirty.

They both smile.

I'm going to have another *limoncello*. It's the liqueur of Sicily, don't ya know?

Lori It's the liqueur of fall-down drunks.

Suzette It's a social error to drink it in a wine glass. *Limoncello* should always be drunk in a shot glass.

Lori So this trip has taught you something.

Suzette Bliss, isn't it?

Lori Yes. Bliss.

Suzette stretches back. Lori reaches out and takes her hand. She holds it for a moment.

Suzette Are you out of love with him?

Lori What a question.

Suzette It's fair to ask.

Lori Mike's been my whole life.

Suzette And that's not an answer.

Lori I've been drifting away from him. I can't help myself. He does things to please me, not because he wants to. Where's the future in that?

Suzette I wouldn't mind.

Lori What?

Suzette Someone who wanted to please me. I could live with that. Most def.

Lori smiles.

Lori Probably we married too young. I was angry.

Suzette Why were you angry?

Lori A heap of things. Because I couldn't play the music I heard in my head.

Suzette sneaks a look at her, then gets up to refill her glass.

What about tomorrow? What's happening tomorrow?

Suzette What's happening tomorrow is the boy in the tight trunks is going to realise he's misjudged his approach.

Lori To his trunks?

Suzette To me.

Lori What's he done wrong?

Suzette Ignored me. When I'm so obviously his future happiness.

Suzette stands, drinking a limoncello.

Mum rang.

Lori Tonight?

Suzette Yes. She had that I-love-you-so-desperately voice. I said, 'Talk normal, Mother. Love isn't a voice.'

Lori Is she coming?

Suzette She's coming when she can.

Lori And when can she?

Suzette When she can.

Lori throws a sideways glance.

Lori And Dad?

Suzette I'm not sure about Dad. I think he'll cut a deal. Like in the movies. I would guess he'll get off on the greater charge of stealing widows' pensions by pleading guilty to the lesser charge of being an all-round dickhead. He'll look great in a suit with arrows. He always looks great.

Suzette looks at her a moment.

What are you going to do?

Lori When?

Suzette When you've stopped what you call looking after me, meaning me looking after you?

Lori Oh . . .

Suzette Go back to teaching?

Lori I'm not sure.

Suzette Why did you stop?

Lori Did I never say?

Suzette Or I wasn't listening.

Lori Because teaching had become nonsense, filling in forms, ticking boxes, manipulating statistics, achieving targets – proving you were doing the job, rather than doing it – I thought, 'All right, if you don't trust me, lose me.' 'If you don't trust anyone but yourselves, lose everyone.' Nobody to do anything because they love it –

Lori hesitates.

I had what I call my Gethsemane.

Suzette What was that?

Lori My moment of doubt. I wondered what on earth I was doing. I locked myself in the staff-room lavatory. And I gave up.

Suzette frowns.

Suzette But that's not Gethsemane.

Lori Why not?

Suzette You mean Gethsemane in the Bible?

Lori Is there another?

Suzette But that's not the story.

Lori Yes it is.

Suzette No it's not.

Lori Christ had a night of doubt.

Suzette Yes.

Lori opens her hands to say, 'That's what it is.'

Lori Gethsemane.

Suzette No.

Lori Why not?

Suzette Because you had a night of doubt and it changed you. You changed direction. You walked away. That's not Gethsemane.

Lori What's Gethsemane?

Suzette Jesus went through with it. Gethsemane's when you have a night of doubt but you go through with it. You go on.

Lori You're right.

There's silence. It has never occurred to her.

You're right.

Suzette You missed the point of the story.

There is another silence, then very quietly.

Duh!

Lori gets up.

Lori I'm going to bed.

Suzette I'm going too.

Lori clears up the things by the chairs.

Could you do me a favour?

Lori What is it?

Suzette Play for me.

Lori No.

Suzette Why not?

Lori No.

Suzette Please.

Lori I don't want to.

Suzette Why not, Lori? Why won't you play?

Lori turns out a few lights. It's near dark.

How much longer do you think we'll stay?

Lori Well, we can't leave.

Suzette Why not?

Lori Because we can't pay the bill. Your mother said she'd pay but it's never come. I guess she'll remember.

Suzette I guess she will.

Suzette stands, wearing sunglasses in the dark.

Hmm. I'm iced, I'm yellow, I'm a living *limoncello*.

Lori Goodnight, Suzette.

Suzette Goodnight, Lori.

Suzette goes.

Goodnight.

Lori Goodnight.

When Suzette is out of earshot, Lori looks at her hands. Then she turns to the table. She starts to mime playing a Beethoven sonata. She begins a couple of times, then her fingers begin to work.

The Beethoven sonata is now heard. The music takes over, and her fingers fly, dexterous, obedient.

Darkness.